# ROADMAP TO
# FINANCIAL
# INDEPENDENCE

## ROBERT BARBERA

THE **M**
MENTORIS
PROJECT

Mentoris Project
745 South Sierra Madre Drive
San Marino, CA 91108

Copyright © 2025 Mentoris Project
Cover design: Karen Richardson

More information at www.mentorisproject.org

ISBN: 978-1-947431-57-7
Library of Congress Control Number: 2025930956

All net proceeds from the sale of this book will be donated to the Mentoris Project whose mission is to support educational initiatives that foster an appreciation of history and culture to encourage and inspire young people to create a stronger future.

Publisher's Cataloging-in-Publication (Provided by Cassidy Cataloguing Services, Inc.)
Names: Barbera, Robert, 1932- author.
Title: Roadmap to financial independence / Robert Barbera.
Description: San Marino, CA : The Mentoris Project, [2025]
Identifiers: ISBN: 978-1-947431-57-7 (paperback) | LCCN: 2025930956
Subjects: LCSH: Finance, Personal. | Investments. | Wealth. | Stocks. |
BISAC: BUSINESS & ECONOMICS / Personal Finance / Investing. | BUSINESS & ECONOMICS / Personal Finance / Money Management. | BUSINESS & ECONOMICS / Investments & Securities / General.
Classification: LCC: HG179 .B37 2025 | DDC: 332.024--dc23

# CONTENTS

# Peace of Mind

We are all on a journey.
We all want to better our lives, attain peace
of mind, and be financially independent.

I believe that investing in our economy can
be rewarding, personally and financially.

Achieving success takes due diligence as well as active
participation. We must continually acquire information,
evaluate risks, and remain vigilant. It takes patience and acumen.

But ultimately, it's not about how much wealth
you acquire, but how you walked the path.

Happiness comes from ourselves.
Each of us makes the final decision on the kind of
life we want to live, the person we want to be.

It's not too late to start today.
There is always time to do the right thing.

# INTRODUCTION

*There is no independence without
financial independence.*

That might sound harsh, but it's true. If you are tied to a paycheck, you're tied to a job—sometimes a very specific job and a specific workplace that might not be the best for you. If you can't afford the security deposit, you might be stuck with a roommate you don't like, or in an apartment that adds an hour to your commute, or in a neighborhood that is becoming unsafe.

Without financial resources, you are yoked to people and situations that may not be ideal, or even defensible.

In one of my early jobs (for a private certified public accountant's office, which I will not name), on my first audit, I was sent to take inventory with the owner's foreman of some oil reserves in an oil field claimed to be owned by our client. I was to calculate gallons of oil by the gauge on the side of the tank pointed out to me.

I had some questions. First and foremost, how could I know if the gauges were accurate? Also, the field contained a few hundred tanks; how could I identify which ones belonged to our client? The foreman—who, of course, was not impartial, since he worked for the client—just shrugged and told me this was how they did it.

The next day I was reprimanded by my boss.

I smelled a fish and left that job. I could do that because I had financial resources: I was skilled and certified in an in-demand profession, so

I knew I would have no trouble finding work. I had an emergency fund to cover immediate needs. We didn't have a family yet, so my wife's job offered us a second stream of income. We didn't yet have the kind of wealth we would go on to create—and that I hope you will be able to create for yourself—but we were financially resourced. Money gave me the freedom to walk away.

If you found yourself in a similar situation, would you be able to walk away?

This is the power of financial independence: At its most basic level, financial independence increases your options. Financial freedom doesn't just offer the ability to leave a situation. Even more powerful is its ability to pull you toward a better future. Financial independence frees you up to focus on what you want to do, where you want to go, who you want to spend time with, and what contribution you can uniquely make in the world. It gives you the bandwidth to not just dream of spending time with loved ones, opening your own business, or writing a book as you travel the world, but also to develop concrete plans to make those dreams come true.

The freedom to create the life you want to live is intrinsically tied to your financial independence.

I have written several books on financial savvy, from my memoir, *Building Wealth*, to my first primer, *Building Wealth 101*, where I lay out both the mindset and multiple strategies to build wealth over time. In *Retire and Refire*, I offer information and roadmaps to people at all stages of life to set themselves up for retirement success. Most recently, in *How to Jump-Start Your Way to Real Estate Wealth*, I pass along a lifetime of lessons in investing in real estate and managing properties. So what is there left for me to teach you?

Financial wealth, that's what.

Financial wealth is money that comes from the financial world. Typically, we think of this as investing in the stock market, but it's much more than that. Furthermore, I have come across many smart people who look at the paper world—including the stock market, lending market, and other financing opportunities—as something mysterious or (worse) as gambling. I won't pretend there aren't risks, but I do believe that "risk" is not the same as "gambling." You take a risk when you cross the street, but not taking it means never leaving the block you were born on. Furthermore, you can avail yourself of traffic lights, pedestrian crossways, looking both ways before you step off the sidewalk, using a crossing guard … you get my point. While there is a certain amount of risk no matter what you do (or don't do) with your money, by taking precautions you can limit risk, just as you would when crossing the street. It is always a case of weighing risks and benefits.

In this book, you will find both risks and benefits on display, my missteps as well as my successes. The important thing, I believe, is not just to learn from your mistakes, but to learn the right lessons. One miscalculation should not result in you deciding you're "bad with money" or that you can never succeed in the stock market or anywhere else. But it should teach you many other things, from understanding your personal tolerance for risk to recognizing the forces that act upon a particular industry or the world economy in general. Be a sponge. Stay open to new information. There is no shame in pivoting when necessary, in taking a new tack if that's what is required to right your financial ship.

In other words, learn—don't judge.

Finally (and I will say this more than once in these pages), this book is not to be taken as investment advice. I'm never going to tell you what you *should* do with your own money. Instead, I will lay out different things you *could* do to build wealth. Everyone is different; you have a different tolerance for risk than I do, entire industries are undergoing disruption and transformation even as I write this, and a stock I like today may not be around by the time you read these words. But fundamentals never change. This book seeks to demystify financial wealth so that you can make a more informed choice about where and why and how you can forge your own path to building wealth. But it is not investing advice, and I will continue to offer you all the disclaimers.

And that's a good thing. The bad news is that you can never follow someone else's path and get the same result. If those days ever existed—and I have my doubts—they are long gone. There are too many variables, and the first and most important one is you. You will succeed in your own way, hopefully learning from the mistakes of others (including me) and bouncing back sooner when you do stumble. If you take nothing else from this book, take this to heart: There is always a way forward. Find it.

I hope your journey to financial success is filled with opportunity.

# PART ONE

## PLAN FOR SUCCESS

# CHAPTER ONE

## A PRIMER ON WEALTH

## The Wealthiest Country

L et's take a broad perspective.

The collective wealth of a nation is measured by all the production and consumption in the economy. In other words, a healthy economy both creates and consumes.

### Productivity

Productivity is the amount of both goods (physical things, from growing tomatoes to making rocket ships) and services (from dog-walking to banking) that citizens of a country produce. In economic circles, it is called the gross national product (GNP). The GNP is very close to the gross domestic product, or GDP; the main difference is that the GNP includes any income our citizens receive from overseas investments. Both measures quantify our nation's wealth, rather than the wealth of any individual person.

From my point of view, production is infectious: The more we produce, the greater our standard of living, and the more inspired we become. We want to produce more and better. The United States is very good at production. We have abundant resources, a creative labor force, and well-educated engineers. I believe that the more invested we are in our economy, the more incentive we have to continue building it with new products and services.

This is one reason why I believe everyone should be invested financially in the country's economy—to bring home this idea that we are all working together for a better future. You are not a cog in the wheel. You are a member of the team.

## Consumption

Consumption probably doesn't need an explanation, but just in case, it's driven by all the stuff we buy. You're a consumer when you consume your breakfast cereal or when you buy a new phone. Your personal, individual preferences in what you consume/purchase drive the market by creating demand for the things you like. When more people want a product, producers work to increase the supply of that product.

You've surely heard the phrase "supply and demand." The push and pull between these two forces (how much there is of something versus how many people want the thing) sets market prices. Pricing is just one of many ways to encourage people to buy or to not buy a thing. For instance, when there is too much of something—say, corn—and not enough demand, the price of corn goes down as a way to encourage people to buy it. Sure, corn might not be something you'd spend $10 on to bring to the barbecue, but maybe it looks more enticing to you when you can get a bag of ears for only $5. At least, that's what the corn growers hope.

It works the other way as well: When more people want to move into a neighborhood than there are houses in that area, they will pay above the asking price. That's when bidding wars happen, and sometimes those higher prices will actually convince someone to sell their house, adding to the number on the market—in other words, increasing supply.

This dance continues, both up and down, all the time. Of course it's a little more complicated: There are bad actors who take advantage either by falsely creating scarcity or otherwise trying to scam people. The government may step in either to manage those bad actors or to artificially make it easier or more difficult to purchase something. And we shouldn't forget that consumers themselves are fickle! Some markets are driven up or down by fads or fears or just plain greed. But in time, people's choices correct the market while consumption and production remain in balance.

## Capitalism

The number of people in our country who are capitalists is more than most people think. It includes people who invest in the stock market either individually, in retirement accounts, or in pensions. Own a small business? Work for yourself? You're a capitalist.

Capitalism is the antithesis of communism. Capitalists own and control the means of production, while in a communist state, only the government owns and controls the means of production. The success of capitalism far exceeds communism in terms of production.

Why? Because people work harder when they have a stake. We want the freedom to create our own destiny.

All activity starts with capital, or money; it is the driving force in our economy. Investments are stored capital, generating more money for you in interest, dividends, increased share value, or a combination of those.

*The most important single central fact
about a free market is that no exchange
takes place unless both parties benefit.*
—Milton Friedman

## Government Wealth

The U.S. government is made up of We the People, for the people. Our government is not expected to be a producer or competitor in the production of goods and services. Rather, it provides the people of the country with the things we need to keep the country together, such as roads, bridges, and other infrastructure for the common good; public schools to ensure an educated populace; and a standing military to provide for the country's safety. Government agencies oversee, protect, and/or regulate a plethora of things (oil production, farming, food) and professions (contractors, attorneys, doctors). There are agencies ensuring fairness, such as the Office of Weights and Measures, which makes sure that both buyers and sellers are measuring the same way—apples to apples, rather than apples to hippos. Building and safety regulations protect construction so that dangerous corners aren't cut, while the Environmental Protection Agency assures safe water and air, the highway patrol keeps traffic flowing, and the judicial courts interpret the law the same way for everyone. There is great value in uniformity, in fairness, and in the ability to depend upon a baseline of safety. We appreciate it as human beings, and because financial markets are driven by human beings, the markets appreciate it as well.

I am not anti-government. I believe in the government's role to keep us secure and to regulate as needed in the public's interest. There are plenty of bad actors in the world, both foreign entities and our own citizens, who violate our laws. As scams become increasingly complex, the bureaucracy needed to manage the burden of protecting us from scams continues to grow. But just because I don't love bureaucracy doesn't mean I don't see the need for it. It would be much worse to allow people like Bernie Madoff to run amok and wipe out people's life savings, or companies like Theranos to dupe investors with impunity.

As I travel around the world and visit other countries, I come to appreciate the United States even more. Our infrastructure is far ahead in terms of roads, bridges, waterways, and highways. The government is involved in innumerable areas to protect its citizens in manufacturing, hospitals, shopping centers, food safety, child safety, and creating educational facilities, not just for K-12, but also for colleges and universities. I am proud of our continued investment in our citizens. Our economy is dependent on safe roadways, convenient distribution of goods, and an educated workforce. It's right that we all share in the costs of these underpinnings of our society.

*Europe was created by history.*
*America was created by philosophy.*
—Margaret Thatcher

That said, there are negative outcomes of government as well. The average tax burden is rising; whereas in 1940, it took sixty-six days of working to pay off one's taxes, today it takes an average of 106 days (per the Tax Foundation, a think tank in Washington, D.C.). The average person's tax burden has risen from 18 percent of their income to 29 percent. That's a tremendous weight on working people, cutting into the amount they themselves can invest in our country, build their own wealth from, and save to take care of themselves and their loved ones in retirement.

While bureaucracy may be necessary, it doesn't necessarily have to be as convoluted and expensive as it is. Reasonable people can disagree on where government funds should or shouldn't be allocated. And I used to work for the Internal Revenue Service (IRS). I know firsthand how adding rules and regulations to the tax code puts pressure on citizens.

Our economy is complex. Even our brightest, most experienced minds don't always understand the ramifications of regulations or other steps that might seek to drive an industry or even our entire economy up or down. Increasing government debt, for instance, may have an immediate impact on the economy, but it can also have a long-term negative price to pay. And as we've sadly learned, even good-faith efforts can be co-opted by greed.

I don't believe there's a magic bullet to perfectly regulate any economy, but I do think it behooves every investor to learn basic economic theory so they can make informed decisions on their investments in particular, and understand the market at large.

As an investor, it is vital for you to know if a regulatory agency or a new rule or a rate hike is beneficial or detrimental to your investment. The government is our silent partner, providing infrastructure, services, and protection. In exchange, that silent partner collects taxes. Business decisions should always be made by taking tax implications into account. As someone who worked for the IRS, I believe in everyone paying their fair share, but that doesn't mean you need to pay above and beyond. Tax codes were built to create incentives; there is nothing wrong with taking those into account when you contemplate investments. Again, it is up to you to be an active participant in our country and our economy.

As a democracy, we have a say in our government, and with that comes the responsibility to understand the role of government in keeping our country organized, protecting our security, and maintaining our quality of life, including the costs associated with these and other government decisions. I welcome criticism of the government when it comes from caring, from wanting to see the government do better for everyone. I don't think anyone will be surprised to know that I appreciate our capitalist system and am against government interference in the market, particularly the types of government activities that go on in communist countries in an attempt to control not just their economies, but their citizens as well. In fact, I believe our market economy offers everyone a chance to participate in the wealth of our country. That is a strength, not a weakness.

> *After the Constitution was signed, Elizabeth Willing Powel asked Benjamin Franklin, "Well, Doctor, what have we got? A republic or a monarchy?" Ben Franklin replied: "A Republic, if you can keep it."*
> —Reported by James McHenry

I believe we will keep it.

## Individual Wealth

After World War II, in the late 1940s and early 1950s, the middle class became more significant. Women went into the workplace in greater numbers, and with that second income, the standard of living changed. New appliances reduced housework, families acquired second cars and bigger houses, people ate out more often and went on more vacations. Education grew in importance; you no longer could get into many professions with just a high school degree. Wardrobes, hair grooming, health insurance, early retirement . . . daily life required more of an investment on every level.

According to the U.S. Census Bureau, in 1960, the median household income was $5,600. Forty years later, it was $42,148. By the 2020s, the median household income reached $74,580. Households with two wage earners now average around $120,000 per year, with 65.6 percent of working women now working full-time year-round. Our grandparents could never have imagined the standard of living we currently enjoy.

The minimum wage has gone up, there is free public education, and amenities our grandparents never dreamed of, such as television and cell phones, have become available to the average person. With longer life expectancy, individuals have more years to create wealth; many will pass that wealth along to the next generation, which (I hope) will be able to live even longer lives. More blue-collar workers have entered the stock market, if only through their pensions or IRA savings accounts. Ideally, we are all benefiting from our country's economic growth.

The key is, once our basic needs of food, clothing, shelter, and transportation have been met, to start investing our savings to get the most financial growth—for ourselves and to pass along to the next generation.

Let's get started.

# CHAPTER TWO

## START PLANNING TODAY

Nobody plans to fail. They just fail to plan. When it comes to plan-ning for the future, mistakes are inevitable. No one has a crystal ball; no one is able to foresee all the possible problems, challenges, or even victories. But you must not let that stop you from making—and following—a plan.

## An Incomplete Plan Is Better than No Plan at All

Let me tell you a story. When I was first married, my late wife, Bernice, and I lived in a house we rented from a man named Mr. Anderson. We lived in the house behind his, and every day, when I was on my way to class (I was in my first year of college at Los Angeles City College), I would see him relaxing or going for a walk, or maybe chatting with friends. Finally, I worked up the courage to ask him how that was possible. When did he go to work?

"Robert," he told me, "I don't go to work anymore. The rent you pay and the rent my other tenant pays me, that's enough for me to live on. I don't have to worry about making money. I can spend my days doing what I love."

To say I was taken aback would be an understatement. I had never imagined such a thing. Mr. Anderson's way of life was a revelation to me.

I talked to Bernice about it right away. "How can we do what Mr. Anderson is doing?" I asked her.

Bernice was Mexican American and we thought we might want to live in Mexico, so we did some research, found out how much money we needed each month to live well there (it was between $350 and $500; this was in the early 1950s), and figured out what we needed as a nest egg to get us that much money in interest from our savings account.

At the time, the interest rate was higher than it is now (our savings and loan was giving us something like 5 percent, if I remember right), so the math wasn't complicated. We realized that if we continued saving as we were doing, we'd have enough money to generate that amount of interest by the time I was 40, which sounded much better to me than working until I was sixty-five. That was our first plan: We were going to build a savings account balance that would give us $500 per month in interest income, move to Mexico, and retire so we could do whatever we wanted all day long.

It had some flaws in it, that plan; quite a few hiccups, in fact, which I'll talk about as we go on. But it had one golden benefit that more than balanced out all its shortcomings—it pointed us in a clear direction. It marshaled our efforts toward a well-defined, compelling goal: financial freedom.

> *Wealth, like happiness, is never attained when sought after directly. It comes as a by-product of providing a useful service.*
>
> —Henry Ford

## How Much Money Do You Need to Be Wealthy?

You may think that you want to live like the cartoon character Scrooge McDuck and take a daily dive into a pool of gold coins, but

I'm going to suggest that fantasy deserves a deeper look. Above a certain level of financial security, more money does not make human beings significantly happier.

There have been lots of studies done on lottery ticket winners and happiness, and they've all found the same thing: There is an initial bump, an increase of happiness, when someone wins the lottery, but within a few months, they go back to their initial, pre-lottery level of happiness.

Look, I would be thrilled for you to become a multimillionaire and test this out for yourself, but I can tell you it's certainly been true in my own life. I remember the day Bernice and I broke the million-dollar income level for the first time. The truth was it snuck up on us. We were so busy with our lives, raising our kids, managing the apartments we owned (I mowed the properties' lawns myself on the weekends). It wasn't until I was doing the books one night that I realized, hey, we had finally hit an annual income of a million dollars. And you know what? The next day, we got up and kept on doing the work. It didn't change our lives or our happiness level.

I'm not trying to burst your bubble. I think this is actually great news: It means you don't have to wait until you're a millionaire to be happy. In fact, you get to be happy along the way. One of the things that makes us happy is striving for and achieving meaningful goals. Setting meaningful goals that will help you reach your ultimate goal of financial independence allows you to feel good again and again as you reach each one. And having a specific end goal helps keep you focused.

So, let's figure out what the finish line is. How much money a year would you need to live your ideal life?

Mr. Anderson needed the income from two income-producing properties to cover his needs and his greatest desire, which was to relax and hang out with his family and friends. Bernice and I originally planned for what we would need financially to be able to live a great life in Mexico. You may want to travel the world or fund a nonprofit. Whatever your dreams are, attaching a number to them will help you get there. Remember, an imperfect goal is still better than no goal at all.

If you think your goal is to have, say, a private jet and eat all your meals on gold-plated dishes, let me suggest you rethink your goals.

Look, if you're a pilot and having a private jet means you can fulfill your lifelong dream of flying to every country in the world, maybe that makes sense. I won't try to stop you. But you can see how that's a very different reason for wanting a jet than simply owning a jet as a status symbol.

Look for the goal underneath the thing you think you want. I've never been one to advocate for conspicuous consumption. In fact, I've given lectures where I've had people cut up their credit cards right there! "Keeping up with the Joneses" is poison to your future wealth; it prevents you from building your investment portfolio. When Bernice and I were just starting out, we enjoyed free concerts in the park, long walks, home-cooked meals, and watching television. We were never caught up in spending money because other people did, and what we found was the joy and pride of building that pot of money that we quickly put to work for us . . . that was worth far more than the newest car or a night out on the town.

> *That man is richest whose pleasures are cheapest.*
> —Henry David Thoreau

Look at your goals and think about how you want them to make you feel. Aren't there other ways you can get that feeling of pride or of success? Can you get it from the difference you're making in your own life, in the lives of your family, or in the world, rather than from the stuff you own? Are you really free if you're constantly comparing yourself to others?

How much do you actually need each year to live the life you want?

If you truly have no idea, let me give you some parameters. According to the U.S. Census Bureau, the median household income in the United States was $74,580 in 2022, so around $75,000 per year. How does your current income (from your job[s] and the interest or dividends from whatever assets you currently have) stack up to this? Does your current income allow you to live the life you want? Does it give you the freedom to spend your time working on things that give your life meaning and joy?

What you're looking for now is a number that reflects what your ideal spending would be for a year. It sounds simplistic, but it's worth saying: All you need for financial freedom is to reliably have MORE money coming in than going out. So don't think of it in terms of being a millionaire or billionaire—a lot of that money might be in assets you can't easily touch.

Financial independence is having a reliable, repeatable income that is just above what you need to live your ideal life. What is that number?

Congratulations! You now have a goal.

There are lots of ways you can get there. Mr. Anderson reached his with rent income from two tenants. Bernice and I planned to reach ours with simple compound interest. But before you can figure out how you're going to get where you want to go, you have to take stock of where you are now.

# You Are Here

When you look at a map at places like shopping malls or nature trails, you will invariably see a big marker that clearly states "You Are Here." And that is valuable information. How can you figure out how to get where you want to go if you don't know where you are?

So where are you?

When I sat down with Bernice and tried to replicate Mr. Anderson's success, we were just starting out. Bernice and I had recently married. She worked full-time (and was amazing at everything she did) while I completed my college degree. After that, I worked a day job while she took care of our family and, as our real estate holdings increased, kept the books for our growing business. We were partners.

There's a lot you can learn from my own situation, so keep reading.

## Invest in Yourself

Attaining my college degree was the first milestone in our financial success. I started working right out of high school (actually, I started working years earlier, first as a shoeshine boy, but that's a story you can read about in my first book, *Building Wealth*). I noticed that my colleagues with college degrees made more money than I did, even though we did the same kind of work. Opportunities for advancement were also more difficult to come by with just my high school diploma. For me, getting that college degree was foundational.

What is foundational for you in your career?

I know this is a book about making money in the financial world, but you need money to make money. Earning top dollar at your day job helps you build the pool of money you will use to invest. Some people disdain day jobs. Not me. Not only do I think you should have a day job, but I also think you should get paid as much as possible for your labor. Because that is money you can parlay into a diversity of other investments. If there's a credential or a skill set that would be valuable to your employer (or other employers in your field), helping you earn promotions and raises or move to a better-paying company, it behooves you to get it.

> Education has been a mainspring for our
> democracy and freedom, a means of providing
> gifts of knowledge and opportunity to all citizens,
> no matter how humble their background, so they
> could climb higher, help build the American Dream,
> and leave a better life for those who follow.
> —Ronald Reagan

My parents had worked hard to buy their own clothing factory. Before the Great Depression, my dad was riding high, like there was no tomorrow. But he had no backup plan, nothing put away for the future. When the Depression hit, we lost our clothing factory. My dad was a smart guy and very talented at what he did, but he didn't have enough experience or education to know how the stock market really worked, or that the economy would eventually bounce back. We lived from hand to mouth all through the Great Depression. From the experience of those tough years, I was determined to have a better life for my own family.

What does this have to do with you earning top dollar?

Wallace Stevens was a poet at night and on weekends. During the workweek, he was an executive at an insurance company. This job gave him the freedom to do his art and not have to worry about how he would provide for his wife and daughter, even through the Great Depression. Ultimately, he won the Pulitzer Prize as a poet. Would he have been able to attain such success as a poet if he'd been struggling like we were to put food on the table? Maybe, but maybe not having to worry about such things allowed his talent to flourish.

You are investing in yourself by reading this book. Learning a new skill, doubling down on your talents, networking, educating yourself on financial opportunities . . . these can all move the needle. Be intentional; just like with money, you need to get a return on investment (ROI) from your *time*.

Identify what has the most impact. Focus your resources. Get the most bang for your buck (and your time/energy).

## Identify Impact

Identifying what creates the most impact is the same philosophy I used when I started managing apartment complexes. I asked questions, I paid attention, and I put together a list of extras that made potential tenants more interested in renting one apartment over another. What did they value? Windows and parking spaces were critical (you can't reliably rent out a windowless apartment, for example), but things like freshly painted common areas, clean laundry facilities, and great landscaping attracted those willing to pay top dollar.

What creates the highest return on your investment in yourself?

## Know Thyself

To recap, start by taking a good, hard look at where you are. Set an intention that gets you started. For me, that first step was maximizing my earning potential in my field, which was finance and accounting. Once I accomplished that, I needed a new goal, and that is where Mr. Anderson's lifestyle shone like a beacon. I had learned how to read contracts at my mother's knee. If Mr. Anderson and my mother could be landlords, why not Bernice and me? We wouldn't have to wait as long to retire. Buy some property, get a couple of long-term tenants, quit my day job, live the good life. Simple, right?

I hope you're laughing at that, because it makes me laugh at myself thinking about it. But I did promise to be as honest about my missteps as I am about my successes. And this obviously was not nearly as simple as it looked to me at the time.

The problem with this initial plan was not, however, that I was naively optimistic about the amount of money we could make; on the contrary, my first wife and I exceeded all our financial goals before Bernice passed away. No, the problem was that I was completely wrong about what made me happy. One of my first mistakes was not understanding myself and the role my personality played in my financial decisions.

It took me a long time to realize that I am, by nature, restless. I do best when I am challenged. Time and time again as I moved through my careers—note the plural—I started at the bottom. This was often on purpose; I wanted to learn how and why different types of businesses succeed. Each time, as I made a transition from one career to the next, I carried that knowledge with me. My successes and failures in one arena were invaluable lessons that made my next career go more smoothly.

Since I thrived when given a challenge, sometimes I created challenges, choosing ambitious goals as ways to stretch myself. In fact, the first property Bernice and I bought was supposed to be a duplex . . . and then I started running the numbers for a four-unit building . . . but the more we looked at potential properties, the more I realized how much sense it made to buy an eight-unit complex instead. Bernice was a whiz with numbers, and to her it was clear that there was simply no way we could afford an eight-unit place. It was impossible.

I said, "Watch me."

Meeting the challenge was itself fulfilling for me, and that is the lesson here. (NOTE: The lesson is *not* that you have to extend yourself financially to the limit; that is never the lesson!) What is fulfilling for you? It took me a while to realize that decisions aren't just made by looking at numbers. Yes, numbers matter. Be book-smart about your investments—run all the numbers, imagine the worst-case scenario, never leap before you look. But you must also realize that your own personality is going to play a role in your decision-making. Recognizing that early allows you to take that into account. Play to your strengths; don't fight against them.

Most books on financial literacy invite you to take stock of your current financial situation. I agree that is very important. But I also want you to take stock of yourself. What makes you happy? If you have a free afternoon, do you spend it hanging out with friends, like Mr. Anderson did? Or building furniture that you sell on Etsy? Tending to an herb garden? My weekends were spent doing maintenance on our rental properties; it was a family business, and we got the whole family involved. Even now, I'm ninety years old, ostensibly retired, but look at me—I'm writing my fifth book to help people build wealth, and I'm loving every minute of it.

There is no right or wrong answer for you, but there is a true answer. And if you know yourself well, you can know what you really want financial freedom to bring you.

Mr. Anderson was perfectly content with owning two properties and having two sets of tenants. It was enough to meet all his needs; the freedom he desired wasn't to travel the world, but to cultivate friendships and enjoy a life free from having to work for someone else. I ended up owning apartment complexes totaling 500 units, and for much of that time, I held another full-time job. I would have gone crazy trying to live in the aimless, relaxed way that Mr. Anderson so enjoyed. It was more than just the fact that I do best when challenged: I loved the thrill of making big dreams come true, and I found great personal fulfillment in managing clean, respectable homes for so many families.

What does your flavor of financial freedom look like?

Be as honest as you can. When I thought of emulating Mr. Anderson, I wasn't being dishonest, I was just mistaken. I was young and I didn't yet understand what drove me. But learn from that mistake, as I did. Dig a little deeper.

Having said that, don't wait to have all the answers before setting your first goal. You will refine the goal, as we did, when you have better data, but for now, make your best, most honest guess. If all your financial needs were met, what would you really do with your time?

## Scam Alert!

We know to be wary of opportunities that are clearly high-risk, but by the same token, be very, very wary of anyone who tries to tell you that an investment opportunity has no risk at all. They may be trying to manipulate your emotions, tapping into your desire for safety, to hide the fact that it's all a scam.

Every investment carries a certain amount of risk; someone telling you otherwise should be an immediate red flag.

I met a lady in the catering business who worked hard for her money—and who lost her entire nest egg to Bernie Madoff's Ponzi scheme. She had to start all over. It can happen to anybody.

## Understanding Your Risk Tolerance

Let's look at the next important factor you bring to the table: your tolerance for risk. Knowing your personal tolerance for risk is essential to developing a strategy for building wealth.

While it is possible to increase (or decrease) your risk tolerance over time, you have to start where you are. Jumping into a situation that you unconsciously consider to be unacceptably risky can lead you to make terrible choices once you're committed. Don't let anyone—including me—talk you into investing in something you believe to be too risky for your peace of mind. (Reminder: Don't let me talk you into any investment! The goal of this book is to demystify financial wealth, not offer specific investment advice.)

I had a colleague once who ran home every day to read *The Wall Street Journal*. He wanted to check how his portfolio was doing. The only thing was, it was a purely imaginary portfolio. He never bought a single stock. He did pretty well, too! I asked him why he didn't open a real account; he obviously knew what he was doing. But he replied that he didn't gamble. This was just his hobby, and he enjoyed it because there was no monetary pressure. Which is true . . . but there was also no monetary reward.

The problem with assessing risk is that we're pretty bad at it. We, as human beings, are more averse to losing something than we are to NOT gaining something. Which makes no sense, but there are many studies backing it. What it comes down to is that we're more afraid of taking action when there is any chance that we might lose money than we are of taking no action at all, *even when doing nothing means there is a 100 percent chance of not making any money*. And when it comes to money, zero gain actually translates to a *loss* because of inflation.

Case in point: I have some friends who are great savers. They don't go so far as to stuff their savings in their mattresses, but they might as well. Merely putting your money into a savings account is not a path to growth. What these people fail to see is that the money you have today will not be worth the same amount tomorrow, or next year, or in fifty years. Inflation inevitably eats away at your purchasing power.

According to the U.S. Census Bureau, three-quarters of all American families—31 million of them—lived on $5,000 a year or less in 1950. Only 3 percent of American families lived on $10,000 a year or more. What was an elite annual income seventy-five years ago wouldn't even cover a year's rent in most of the country today. Sticking your savings in anything that earns you less interest than the rate of inflation—whether it's a piggy bank or a savings account—means you are LOSING money. Your purchasing power is going down faster than your savings balance is going up.

People sometimes erroneously think they will need less money in retirement than they do now, while they're still working. Disabuse yourself of that notion right now. Sure, you may no longer need a professional wardrobe, but there are other things you might want to spend money on. Many retirees look forward to traveling, for instance, or to spending more time (and money) on a hobby. No matter how good your health insurance may be, you may have costs associated with medical or other quality-of-life issues as you get older.

It is not my place to make your decisions for you (see again all my disclaimers—this book is meant to offer up possibilities, not give you any sort of specific financial advice), but you must understand that if you value security to such an extent that you refuse to take any risk with your money in order to earn a higher-than-inflation return, you are going to need to make some hard decisions now so that you can save as much as humanly possible. It is an uphill battle to attempt to finance what I hope will be decades of healthy, enjoyable retirement just from a savings account alone.

By the same token, it is very difficult to build wealth on a paycheck alone, especially a single paycheck (more on exposure and diversification later). You need to leverage your money in some other way, and that way must return more on your investment than the rate of inflation.

In other words, your money has to work for you, and work hard.

> *Nothing will come of nothing.*
> —William Shakespeare

What does this have to do with risk tolerance?

Generally speaking, the higher the risk of losing your investment, the higher the potential reward. That's pretty straightforward. Once you understand that doing nothing with your money—or putting it somewhere where its earning power is limited to a return below the rate of inflation—is ALSO risky (in fact, it's a guaranteed loss of purchasing power), you can nudge your tolerance for risk up a notch. You can get yourself in the game, not to gamble, but to make informed choices that can help you accumulate wealth over the long term.

I want you to be aware of your innate risk tolerance so you can make decisions you can live with, and so you can understand what is truly risky and what is not, at least when it comes to your investments. Understanding the reasons behind why you choose to make a financial decision will help you make decisions better—and possibly make better decisions. I want you to remember that choosing *not* to take action is itself an action. We can't escape having to make decisions with our lives and our money, but we do better when we align them with who we are as people, our core values, and our life goals.

My mother and father are a good example of this. Where Bernice and I were a partnership, both working toward the same goal, my parents had different goals in life. More importantly, they had different levels of risk tolerance. My mother was very ambitious. She would set a goal, reach it, and use it to leapfrog to a bigger goal. Sometimes it worked out and sometimes things got tough. When I was a kid, we ended up selling our house and moving into one of my mother's apartments; this was after she parlayed a sewing job where she was paid by the piece into buying a vacant lot, building one duplex, then another and another, selling and buying until she owned a 60-unit apartment building in Brooklyn. There were constant challenges—the Great Depression, lawsuits, avaricious partners, bad lawyers, tenants who didn't want to pay rent—but my mother had a voracious capacity for risk. Every setback led to her regrouping and rebuilding.

My father, on the other hand, had much less tolerance for risk. He was incredibly successful and sought-after in his field of fashion design. He had started in the business by sweeping factory floors and worked his way up to the height of the industry. He made enough money working during "the season" that he was able to take more than half the year off entirely. Where my mother was happiest in a tense negotiation, my father was at peace listening to opera and sipping wine. Where risk energized my mother, it ate away at my father, and ultimately, while they remained married, they had to separate.

Whether you are choosing business partners or life partners, you should take into account the capacity you each have to tolerate risks. It's not that one of you is right and the other is wrong; it's that as human beings we make different decisions when we're afraid than we do when we're not. Understanding your own and other people's risk tolerance allows you to understand why they do what they do, possibly anticipate potential problems before they become dire, and in general make better decisions. All of which will help you make money no matter what you do.

One way to balance return on investment with less risk (not "no risk"—remember not to trust anyone who tells you there's no risk!) is to plan to get rich *slowly*.

## What Is Inflation?

Inflation is what we call it when the cost of goods and services increases over time. That rate varies tremendously. According to the U.S. Bureau of Labor Statistics, the average rate of inflation was 3.4 for the year 2000, 0.1 for 2015, and a whopping 8.0 for 2022. As I write this, the average rate of inflation is 2.9 (July 2024).

Practically speaking, it means that a loaf of bread cost $0.28 in 1974, and now in 2024—fifty years later—that same loaf of bread would cost about $1.83. In other words, if you're on a fixed income, your money will buy less and less over time. You must take this into account as you plan your future

## Get Rich Slowly

Do not try to get rich quickly.

The level of risk involved in "get rich quick" schemes is tantamount to gambling. Not necessarily because of the opportunity itself, although many are either cons or actual gambles, but because of the psychology behind the "get rich quick" mindset. We are tempted to put our money on the long shot at the horse race for a number of reasons. Maybe we believe we know more about the horses/racecourse/jockeys than anyone else. Perhaps we get swept up in the idea of a big payout. Or we need a big payout to cover other debts; merely doubling our stake wouldn't be enough. Or someone else convinces us that everyone (or the "right" everyone) is betting on that horse, or we are actively seeking out the elation that can come from taking a huge risk.

Arrogance, naivete, desperation, greed, following the crowd, seeking emotional highs . . . all of these are the wrong reasons to bet on a horse, and they are the wrong reasons to make an investment.

Here's a lesson you can learn from my mistakes. Very early on in life, before I married Bernice, I started day trading on the stock market. I did pretty well, winning more than losing, and yes, I'm using that language—the language of gambling—deliberately. Every day before going to work, I would stop in at a broker and make day trades. It was exciting! I had visions of getting rich quickly. You know how this is going to turn out, right? One day, the market dropped. I had a margin call, and the broker sold the stock. I was pretty much wiped out in that one transaction.

So much for day trading.

You should take note of the lesson I learned from this. I did NOT learn to never invest in the stock market. That would have been the wrong lesson, though it may be the first one to spring to mind. What I learned was to not GAMBLE on the stock market. Don't use it to get a little excitement in your life. Don't expect to get rich in one fell swoop. It can be hard to resist. The energy of the stock market is amazing; the potential for growing your wealth is absolutely there, and it is easy to get caught up in the excitement of the moment, in the frenzy.

But that day taught me that I was going about it the wrong way. I needed to learn how the market worked. I needed to learn from people who were smart and experienced stock market professionals, just as I learned how to read contracts and negotiate deals from my mother. And I needed to start from the bottom, like my father, and work my way up.

Let me take this moment to say what an amazing country we live in, where all of this is even possible. I remember my mother saying, "Only in America!" And it's true. We have a freedom denied to so many others, and that is the opportunity to make our own lives better. To be the people we want to be. I have so many friends from other countries who remain skittish; they don't dare to take risks, to invest, even to build anything because they are afraid it will be taken from them. I've never had that fear. Born in America, I very much appreciate our legal system, our rights of property, our ability to be active participants in the market and not just cogs in a machine. Are there problems with the system? Of course. But we continue to work them out. And no other system offers the same freedom of opportunity, allowing people to build bigger lives than the one they were born into.

> *The essence of America, that which really unites us, is not ethnicity or nationality or religion. It is an idea. And what an idea it is: that you can come from humble circumstances and do great things.*
> —Condoleezza Rice

My mother was right. Only in America.

# CHAPTER THREE

## A QUICK PRIMER ON THE STOCK MARKET

### Forces in the Market

The economy is not the same as the stock market, but it is often reflected in the stock market. What do I mean by that? Technically, the economy could be doing poorly, with flat wages, inflation, a lot of people out of work, and the stock market could still be going up. It doesn't often happen that way, but it could, because the stock market reflects how much people—hundreds of thousands of people—believe in the future of around 2,400 listed companies over the long term. Even something as consequential as the coronavirus pandemic in 2020 didn't have as much impact on stock prices as you would have thought, especially long-term.

The activity of the stock market is tremendously complex; it isn't just world events that need to be taken into account, but also the decisions and, yes, sometimes whims of individuals making decisions, both within companies and as buyers, sellers, and traders of stock. Any situation may or may not affect another part of the economy, which may or may not cause a ripple effect as job reports, earnings, projections, fads, even the weather work for and against each other to influence the price of not just one stock, but the entire market.

*One of the funny things about the stock
market is that every time one person buys,
another sells, and both think they are astute.*

—William Feather

Generally speaking, the economy has two movements: Either the momentum is trending down, indicating a bear market, or trending up, indicating a bull market. It's helpful to think of these not just as trends, but as a cycle. What goes up must come down, and what goes down will, historically, eventually go up. This is NOT true for individual stocks, by the way; some of those go down and go bankrupt. You can lose everything, and we'll go into how to plan for that later. But so far, it has been true that the U.S. stock market as a whole over its history has gone up more than it has gone down.

The thing to remember is, you have to treat each cycle differently. It's not that you will automatically make money in a bull cycle and lose it in a bear cycle. It is easier to make money when the entire stock market is going up, I'll grant you that, but if you only buy when the market is high and only sell in a panic when the market is low . . . well, that is the opposite of "buy low, sell high," which is the one piece of advice everyone feels confident giving.

## What Is a Bear Cycle?

A *bear cycle* occurs when there is an overall declining value in stock. There are many forces in play that can lead to a bear cycle, including:

- Overextended production, such as housing or cars or anything that creates over-built inventory. Producers are on a roll to produce, and there are times when they don't know when to stop, oversaturating the market. When there is too much of something, it means there is more than people want to buy. The very definition of "supply and demand" leads to prices going down when there is too much inventory.

- Overpricing of the stock market itself. Traders and stock buyers show too much exuberance, maybe by trying too hard to "get in on the game," maybe seeing value where there isn't any, in hopes that they can gain even more profit. This can sometimes be referred to as a bubble, with prices getting more and more inflated until the bubble finally bursts. When that happens, entire industries can "correct"—or go down—and that can have a ripple effect on the entire market.

- World events such as wars, epidemics, and natural catastrophes shock the economy, freezing opportunity.

- Manipulation of the stock market by unscrupulous investors creating a false frenzy, making it seem like something is a better investment than it is so they can make a killing by selling their shares before reason sets back in.

- Political disruption by setting rules and regulations to manage the economy. Sometimes these will help the stock market, and other times, they will slow it down.

## Conclusion of a Bear Market Cycle

Here's the bad news: A bear cycle can go on for months or even years until there is a correction of the issues causing the cycle. But that doesn't mean you can't continue to build wealth in a down market. Savvy investors may find excessive decreases—in other words, a good deal on a stock that you believe still has the potential to go up solidly when the market improves. There are opportunities in a bear cycle to buy good stocks for a great price. And there will be stocks that you may have invested in that continue to go up even in a bear market, companies that buck the trend. Inherently, many industries thrive as some industries lose.

Your job is to be proactive.

You cannot change the cycle, but you can take steps to limit your losses. I have an entire section coming up devoted to diversification, and I encourage you to diversify not just your stock market investments, but also your streams of income. But the most important thing for any investment is not to live in a fantasy land. There is an old adage: "Don't bury your head in the sand." While ostriches may not actually do that (despite many cartoons to the contrary), human beings make a grave mistake when they think the next upswing is right around the corner.

Don't ignore the signs of a downturn. Move some of your assets into safer investments and wait for the market correction. Sooner or later, bad times run their course. Don't lose hope and panic-sell! That is not the same thing as taking thoughtful, precautionary measures to make sure you have working capital during the downturn. Eventually, the circumstances that influenced the market to go down level off and the market does get better. Or at least it always has so far.

To me, this is one of the amazing things about America: We're optimists, and we're right to be optimists. When things are good, they are very good, and when they are bad, we work to make them better. The very foundation of our economy supports this constant building and rebuilding. And so far, we have always come back even stronger than before.

> Stock market corrections, although painful
> at the time, are actually a very healthy part
> of the whole mechanism because there are
> always speculative excesses that develop,
> particularly during the long bull market.
>
> —Ron Chernow

## What Is a Bull Cycle?

No surprise here: If a bear market cycle is when stock prices go down, then a *bull cycle* is when we see stock prices trending upward over a period of time. What this signals is that investors are optimistic about the economy, both in terms of stability and the possibility of growth.

Here are some signs of a bull market:

- Profits of many (or even most) companies increase over prior years.

- Larger dividends are given to stockholders compared to prior years.

- New innovation, be it in technology or in pharmaceutical cures, become available and burst onto the scene, creating a new and eager layer of demand.

- National issues that have been creating uncertainty or concern have been resolved.

*A rising tide lifts all boats.*

I had a conversation once with a stockbroker who was boasting a bit about his stock-picking abilities. I laughed and told him, "Who are you kidding? We're in a bull market. You can pick anything and look good!" He was a good sport and agreed with me.

Although I was joking with him, it does highlight the danger of a bull market: Everything looks good. It's hard to tell which companies are really sound and poised to continue to be a good investment for years to come. I will tell you what I look for in a later chapter, but I will also remind you that you always need to remain vigilant. When horses were the main mode of travel, investing in a company that made carriages was just common sense. But the minute the automobile was invented, the entire horse-and-carriage industry went from being a safe bet to complete extinction in a relatively short time.

You have to be able to keep tabs on what might disrupt a bull cycle. Don't get caught up in the enthusiasm of a bubble, because even bull cycles must come to an end.

## Conclusion of a Bull Market Cycle

In a bull market, euphoria can power rally after rally as investors put their money in stocks, reaching out for good times ahead. Until they don't. There comes a moment, either when something happens in the wider world to cause concern among investors, or a bubble reaches absurd values and common sense reasserts itself, reminding buyers that the share price may no longer reflect the fundamental soundness of a company or industry.

At first, the activity in the market may slow. There may be less volume of trading as anxious buyers sit on the sidelines, unwilling to lose out on potential earnings by selling too soon but afraid of losing what they have if the market begins to drop.

But nervousness is infectious. People want to take action. A single spark of good news can sometimes cause the stock market to recover and go even higher, while other times a spark of bad news can cause it to "correct," or start to decline. Big investors use algorithms to identify trends, and average investors may not catch on to what's happening until there is already a downward trend—just as, in a bear market, large investors can often afford to take a risk and get back into investing before average investors feel comfortable buying again.

That's where I land, by the way. I understand that bull and bear cycles will continue to alternate, and I don't worry too much about it. It has been my policy to not buck the cycle, but flow with the trend. I never went to the extreme in either market. I'm not greedy; when a stock has done well for me but I believe it's starting to be valued higher than its fundamentals warrant, I'll sell it. I don't get upset if it continues to go up for a while longer, because I have made a good profit on it.

Similarly, if a stock I believe in goes down in a bear market, I won't sell in a panic. In fact, I'll look for the price to hit what I believe to be a bargain, and I'll take some of that profit I made in the bull market to buy more shares at low prices in a bear market. This is what is meant by "buy low, sell high," and what it takes is a cool head and an eye always toward buying and holding shares of companies you believe are fundamentally sound.

It's the opposite of gambling, the opposite of that thrill I got from day trading.

It's also the path to wealth.

I don't believe so much in predicting the market as I do in paying attention to continuous trends. Does that make me late to the party? A little. I am careful and avoid exposing myself to a lot of what I consider to be unnecessary risk. It is always prudent to be a little patient, waiting for a measurable trend before taking action, so long as you are not driven by a fear of missing out.

This was my dad's advice, by the way. He was a patient man, and always counseled me to wait. There's a difference between waiting because you are indecisive and waiting while carefully watching, gathering data, and looking for opportunities.

There is also value in standing pat and letting the stock market cycle back up again; remember, buying and (especially) selling create tax consequences, especially if you don't hold the stock for very long before selling. Patience and good tax advice are important to wealth building. While I have little faith in stock-pickers, professionals who are well-versed in economics and tax laws can help you figure out how to keep from being exposed and how to minimize the financial consequences of selling your assets. I don't hesitate to pay for experience and sound advice.

## A Word About Crashes and Panics

Crashes, which have also been called panics, are significant market downturns, often happening very quickly. The sudden, extreme downturn results in panic selling as people try to recoup as much as they can of their investment before it goes even lower. This panicked sell-off further depresses prices, resulting in a large overall decline in the market.

At the time of this writing in 2024, we have had six crashes since 1962.

### 1962  KENNEDY SLIDE

The market was overpriced in 1961, leading to fear and sell-off. The "Slide" was a period of adjustment to overpriced shares. The market peaked and had nowhere to go but down to reality.

## 1987  BLACK MONDAY

There was a significant trade deficit, leading to the value of the U.S. dollar decreasing. Black Monday was an adjustment to balance sales to production on imports and exports. I believe we had to adjust or become beholden on a national level to foreign countries.

## 2000  DOTCOM BUBBLE

Huge investments in startup technology stocks peaked and then crashed.

## 2008  SUBPRIME

This was a combination of overconfidence in the housing market, mortgage lenders who manipulated worthless mortgages so they would seem to have value, and a massive number of subprime mortgage holders who defaulted. For a deep look at what happened, you can read *The Big Short* by Michael Lewis or watch the movie adaptation.

## 2018  CRYPTOCURRENCY

Many cryptocurrencies lost significant value, with Bitcoin ultimately losing 80 percent of its value. The market remains extremely volatile. This is only my opinion, but I feel cryptocurrency was hijacked by a young generation who saw it as a way to become millionaires, only to see it usurped by short sellers. There have also recently been cases of suspected malfeasance, such as with FTX.

## 2020  CORONAVIRUS

Panic selling occurred amid the economic slowdown caused by COVID-19.

Crashes have occurred all over the world from time immemorial. You may have heard of Tulip Mania. This happened back in 1637.

For three years, the price of tulip bulbs, a relatively new product on the market that quickly became a status symbol, had been increasing dramatically, to the point where people were no longer buying tulip bulbs to plant—they were buying them to resell, flipping tulips as some people flip houses, or as day traders may flip stocks today. In fact, most speculators weren't buying real tulips at all, but the promise of tulips after the next growing season.

Of course it couldn't last. At some point, the price of tulips became so absurdly high that no one was willing to buy them. There's some dispute over whether or not this first recorded speculative bubble caused significant damage to the economy, but there's no question a lot of investors went to court trying to enforce contracts when the buyers no longer wanted their tulips at any price. The whole fiasco has become a metaphor for any time a speculative bubble builds up beyond the intrinsic value of a company or industry.

Crashes are by definition bad news, and bad news sells newspapers. Any market slide is well-covered by the media. Sadly, many potential investors are scared off by the reporting and stay out of the market, sometimes forever, because of fear of a crash. We've all heard of people who buried money in their backyard rather than trust the banks after the Great Depression, despite the fact that individual bank accounts are now insured by the federal government (FDIC insured) up to (currently) $250,000. Again, it's a question of accurately assessing risk versus reward.

Sooner or later, the reason for the crash is corrected. I have great faith in both America and Americans, and especially in our ability to solve problems. So far, the market has always recovered and in fact grown in value beyond its previous high. The stock market is a reflection of our economy; we shouldn't sell it short.

On the other hand, we do want to learn from history.

I am always looking for ways to grow my investments and create wealth. On the other hand, I want to protect what I have. I imagine that you and I are in agreement on this. We want to go forward, not backward.

I also try to create a safety bubble for myself and my family, no matter what the investment may be. There is no way for me to change the outside world, but I can take precautions to make sure we get through the hard times. I always have a backup plan.

I invite you to put these measures into place now:

- **Get your credit in order.** Having good credit is critical if you need to borrow cash or get capital for an investment. In addition to doing what you need to do to build your credit rating, you should try to develop relationships with two or three bankers. Who are you already doing business with? Be friendly and scrupulously honest with them.

  There's usually some discretion when it comes to bank loans. I once needed a six-month extension on a million-dollar loan, and I got it, too. I was a good risk: No one had ever needed to foreclose on one of my loans, and I had never misrepresented a situation. People knew my word was good. But what really tilted the scales in my favor was that I knew the bank manager personally; I had brought him a lot of business and real trust had developed between us over the years. Enough that he ignored bank policy and carried my million-dollar loan another six months.

  Relationships are important. Don't neglect them.

- **Get life insurance.** This is nonnegotiable. I'm sorry if you don't want to think about dying, but put your squeamishness aside long enough to make a will and sign up for enough life insurance to keep your family safe if something were to happen to you. Don't try to go it alone; an experienced lawyer will be able to save your family money and hassle by setting up things like family trusts now. Take care of this, set those insurance premium payments on automatic withdrawals, and go back to not thinking about dying for the next eighty years—with the comfort of knowing your family will be protected, just in case.

- **Get health insurance.** Talk to an expert about what other kinds of insurance make sense for your business and personal needs. Do not stint on this.

- **Have a diversity of investments,** both inside and outside of the stock market. This will allow you to wait out a down market. The last thing you want is to be so desperate for cash that you are forced to sell your shares while the market is still low.

- **Develop more than one source of income.** You might get fired from your current job or decide you need to quit. You have more freedom to weather a bad break or make a move that better supports your career if you're not waving farewell to your only source of income.

The more you have a plan in place to weather problems, the more ability you will have to take advantage of opportunities. I have reinvented myself time and again. Knowing that my family was going to be fine no matter what the outcome of any given opportunity might be allowed me to try a lot of different things.

> *Where one door shuts, another opens.*
> —Miguel de Cervantes

In addition to the many jobs I held and the apartment buildings I owned and managed, I invested in stocks. And when the stock market looked like a bad investment to me, I invested in other opportunities. And something always came along!

Over the course of my life, I invested in land where I anticipated the value of the land would increase because of zoning changes. I worked as a go-between, connecting potential business partners and helping them put together the deal for their restaurant, including the land it sat on—my own area of expertise. I lent money to people who were creditworthy but were nonetheless denied by bankers who couldn't see the potential of their businesses. Once, I bought a shipment of imported art paintings that was sitting in a warehouse because whoever had bought the paintings couldn't pay the shipping charges; for the price of the uncollected freight, I had an entire shipment of paintings to resell. I bought gold and silver (although I have a cautionary tale about that later).

Be flexible. Look for opportunities. Recognize that you always have a choice. As profitability in one area, such as the stock market, decreases, look to see what else is doing well. Even within the stock market, some industries will go up as others go down. I had a lot of fun experiences, most of which made me money in the end, because I kept my eyes open, made friends, was curious as to how things worked, asked questions, and took a genuine interest in people's lives.

There's one more thing you need, and that's a real desire to make a change. I had an acquaintance who had gone from being a truck driver to owning a successful trucking business. I was thrilled by his success and genuinely curious about what made him decide to make such a big shift. He told me that when he was in middle age, he had a heart attack. Although he had recovered, he was worried about his family. What would happen to his young daughter if something happened to him? He decided that he was never going to be able to keep her secure financially just by driving a truck, so he gave up his truck job and went into business for himself. He knew the business well, having worked in it from the bottom up, and he had lit a fire under himself: the desire to build something that would continue to support his daughter even if he died.

There it is. When you really want something, when you have a compelling reason, you just go and do it. We are so blessed to live in a country that supports individuals creating their own businesses and building their own futures so that they can care for the people who matter to them.

When you don't give up, you figure it out.

*America is another word for Opportunity.*
—Ralph Waldo Emerson

# The Sweet Spot

Here's what you're going for: You are looking for the day when your accumulated wealth supports you. This is your goal. This is NOT when you have enough money that you think your principal—i.e., the pot of money you have saved up over your years of working—will cover your retirement.

Here's what the (erroneous) math looks like:

- George expects he'll live for twenty years after he retires.
- He wants to have an annual income of $100,000.
- 20 x $100,000 = $2 million

By this math, George needs $2 million in the bank before he can retire. He will spend $100,000 of it every year for the next twenty years, bringing his savings down to zero. At which point, he will conveniently die just as his money runs out.

No. WRONG. That is not how it works. In fact, this is a recipe for disaster. What if George finds himself with a major expense one year? What if he lives longer than 20 years (which we all hope for)? And then there's inflation; that $100,000 will buy less and less each year. Not to mention the anxiety of worrying that he might outlive his savings.

What George should do instead is invest his savings in something that will give him enough of a return on investment that he can rely on the interest and never touch the principal.

*If you don't find a way to make money while you sleep, you will work until you die.*
—Warren Buffett

George will continue to have a similar amount of capital no matter how long he lives and will have no anxiety about being able to enjoy the good life after retiring because that investment money is doing the hard work for him. It is working by being used to build companies (stocks) or government infrastructure (government bonds) or appreciating (real estate). The income it produces for that work is available to

George in terms of interest payments, dividends, equity, and increased stock value.

I call this equilibrium the Sweet Spot.

Here's a real-life example. Forty years ago, I opened an IRA. If you don't know what an individual retirement account is, the quick version is that it's like a piggy bank you can't break open until you're of retirement age. I'm a fan, by the way: It forces you to have patience and view the market as a long-term strategy to build wealth. One of the key benefits is that your money grows tax-free while you're working. Most plans allow you to automatically deposit money every month; set it up once and you don't have to worry about remembering or being disciplined. It easily allows investing to become a habit.

There are different kinds of IRAs and a variety of rules governing how much you can put in and when you can take money out, so talk to a tax professional or your accountant before you set one up.

Back to my IRA. By the time I was of retirement age, I had put about $600,000 in my IRA over the years. But that money wasn't just sitting there—it was invested in stocks. Initially, I was making around a 4 percent to 6 percent return, but the beauty of not being able to touch that money meant that everything compounded. The dividends were reinvested, buying more stock that then generated more dividends. I'm now making a return on investment of 8 percent or more. In addition, stock prices trended up, so the value of the account increased.

When you hit a certain age, you have to start taking withdrawals from your IRA; it's called the required minimum distribution (RMD), and as the name implies, it is mandatory. The amount you need to take out every year varies depending on the value of your IRA, your age, and the expected return on investment. You want to make sure you're taking out the right amount; there are penalties to not taking out enough once you reach (currently) the age of seventy-three. Again, I urge you to talk to a tax professional about this.

When I needed to start taking money out, I withdrew $4,000 every month to cover the bulk of our living expenses. Over the years, I have taken out a total withdrawal of $1,062,728. The current account balance is $1,084,822.

That is what I call a perfect Sweet Spot.

# Chapter Four

## The Four Conditions

Before we get into the nitty-gritty of what a financial plan might look like, let's take a step back and look at the bigger picture. Putting together a plan to meet your financial goals is a key step, but it's not the only step. I believe four conditions are necessary for success. Certainly all four have been necessary for my success. They are:

1. Have a plan.
2. Be productive.
3. Satisfy a purpose.
4. Establish priorities.

Let's look at these conditions one at a time.

## Have a Plan

Putting together a plan for success is a really good place to start. Unfortunately, most of us have no idea what that looks like. We are taught that success looks like working hard and getting good grades. While I am a fan of hard work and lifelong learning, those two skills, alone or combined, are still not enough to build wealth. We're rarely taught, for instance, how to develop a financial plan or investment strategies—something I hope to counter in this book. But it would be great if parents, communities, and schools also offered some practical help beyond the "work hard/get a good education" advice.

My parents were no different; they impressed upon me the importance of both working and studying hard. It seemed that everyone I knew started out with a formal education, perhaps through high school, followed by an education in a profession or trade. They never really talked to me or my brother about financial planning, but their actions provided us with an example and many lessons were absorbed from watching them. My memoir, *Building Wealth*, goes into more detail, particularly on the different philosophies embodied by each of my parents and my brother as well, but there are a few lessons learned that I'd like to share here.

My mother had only a third-grade education; as an Italian immigrant, English was not her first language. It was to fill this gap that I began my own apprenticeship when I was still in elementary school: She would have me read contracts aloud to her. Because my mother— and you will hear more about her later—was not just a very hard worker. She was also a savvy businesswoman. I learned from both her successes and her failures what to look for in a contract and what to be wary of. It was invaluable, particularly because I was able to absorb this knowledge so young and live through the results of this or that financial decision, seeing how it played out in both the short and long terms.

> *In this world nothing can be said to be*
> *certain, except death and taxes.*
> —Benjamin Franklin

> *That may be true, but it doesn't take into account*
> *the joy in making what you can before death, and*
> *estate planning so that you don't have to pay taxes.*
> —Robert Barbera

As I mentioned, I went on to start at the bottom again and again, so that I could learn by watching others, by seeing how all the parts worked (or didn't work) together so that I could identify best practices and potential pitfalls. When they talk about getting an education, they may mean reading, writing, and arithmetic, but once you've got those, it behooves you to get educated about the nuts and bolts of any industry that your livelihood depends upon. The glossy investment pamphlet is not going to get you far; you need to understand the inner workings.

In other words, to put together a solid plan for success, you're probably going to need better data than you currently have.

One way to get data is to read books, of course. (Great job reading this one!) But also find mentors. Talk to people who work in industries you might invest in. Be curious about what your friends do; take them out for coffee and learn from their successes and frustrations. Find ways to get in the game yourself, in small ways. Make mistakes and learn from them. Get better data.

*Failure is the key to success; each*
*mistake teaches us something.*
—Morihei Ueshiba

In the interim, however, go ahead and make a plan now. An imperfect plan is still better than no plan—it gives you something to finesse as you learn more.

For instance, Bernice and I eventually ended up owning 500 apartment units. But that was not our first plan. Our very first plan was probably me bursting in after talking to Mr. Anderson and thinking we only needed to own two or three units. That plan didn't last very long. When we started looking at buying our first investment property, I quickly realized more units meant more stability: If one or two were empty for a short while, we still would have income from the ones that were occupied. If you only have one rental income stream and that tenant leaves, you suddenly have zero money coming in while you fix it up and find another renter. Your income is zero, but your expenses may actually increase in the short term. It was far more prudent to buy a duplex than a single-family home to rent out, and even more prudent to buy a building with more units.

The more I learned, the more I shifted my plan until finally I settled on an eight-unit building for our first major investment. You know how they say two can live as cheaply as one? It was kind of the same with the rental properties: Maintaining a couple of them was not that much more work than maintaining one of them, especially if they weren't too far apart. We continued to upgrade and add to our properties until we had an easy loop we could do on the weekends. I mowed the lawns. It was great!

When we reached 100 units, that's when I sat down to do the real math. From what I'd learned from my mother, who invested in real estate herself, and what I'd learned from acquiring and managing the units we already owned, 500 units seemed to me to be a good number. By this time, we had invested in other contractors to maintain the properties, our family business having outgrown a single family's ability to keep them in shape. I realized we could save money by creating our own management company, and to keep those people employed full-time, a loop of properties with 500 units would be just the ticket. Not so many tenants that it became a soulless machine, but enough to soften any problems with a particular building, or perhaps a slump in the rental market, and to keep our employees fully employed. And that's what we attained; our last property took us just above 500 units.

But if I hadn't had the initial plan to buy a single rental property, I would never have set us on the path to learning about investment properties in the first place. All our success started with a modest plan that pointed us in the right direction. And if it had been the wrong direction, we would have learned from that as well! You need real data to make good decisions, and you only get real data from getting in and trying things.

Start with a basic plan. You already have a notion that you want to build wealth or you wouldn't have picked up this book. We all have a dream of being useful to ourselves, our family, and our community. What does that look like? How much money do you need to make it doable? Put a number to the dream of living exactly the life you want. How much wealth is enough? (Pick something that sounds good; I'll go into my own ideas about your Sweet Spot in a later chapter.)

Then add a date. By when do you want to have this passive income? Let me caution against get-rich-quick schemes. In a casino, the house always wins—and you're never the house. Anything that promises you untold riches is playing on human emotions of either greed or desperation, and neither of those leads to a good outcome for you. The hallmark of the Bernie Madoffs of the world is that they make it look like what they offer is too good to be true—and it usually is. Steer clear.

Now brainstorm about a few ways you might be able to make this dollar amount by the date you chose.

To recap: Pick a reasonable number, a reasonable date, and a couple of ways you think it might happen. Set it aside for now and we'll adjust as we go.

# Be Productive

Multitasking gets a bad rap. I love multitasking. For most of my adult life, I held down a day job while at the same time investing in apartment houses and the stock market. Sometimes, I held down a second job (or a side hustle, as it's called these days) and volunteered my time doing everything from teaching personal finance to publishing books to raising enormous sums for a variety of educational institutions. I love having more than one or two things going on in my life at any given time.

Possibly it all stems from my mother's insistence on being productive.

*Always be a producer.*
—Rose Barbera (my mother)

I can still hear my mother's voice in my head, "Produce! Produce!" in her Italian accent. My mother didn't care what I was doing, so long as I was accomplishing something. She refused to give into laziness herself. As a seamstress in a factory, she was paid by the piece. Even as she ate lunch, she would continue to work on garments. The more items she finished, the more money she made, so wasting time was truly wasting money. The only way to maximize your potential is to give things your all.

This isn't merely true for those who are paid by the finished piece. Even when you are paid a flat salary, giving it your all can help you get ahead. Everywhere I worked, from the IRS to a savings and loan to a restaurant that I co-owned and managed, I took on extra work not only to satisfy my employers, but also for my own personal satisfaction. That extra effort may lead to getting noticed and promoted (and those raises and bonuses should be earmarked for your investment portfolio), but that's not even the real benefit. When you put in that extra effort, you show yourself that you are always capable of more.

That's what will change your life.

As a bonus, you often learn more than you need to know to do the job you were hired for. Which puts you in a good position to move up the ladder, either internally or at another job. Competence is a useful skill.

Why am I talking so much about day jobs when this is a book about financial wealth? Because unless you come from money, which I certainly didn't, you will need the income stream from a day job to help you build your wealth. If you don't have enough money to cover groceries, where will you find the money to invest in the stock market? I wasn't kidding when I mentioned Bernie Madoff; there will always be bad actors who prey on the hopes and dreams of their fellow human beings. Being desperate makes you more vulnerable to such people.

A steady, if boring, stream of income from a day job can support you not just in terms of food and shelter, but it can also prevent you from the desperation that makes you easier prey for scam artists. Just as I wanted to have multiple units to even out the income stream from my rental properties, I also believe in having multiple streams of income, as predictable as possible, from a variety of sources. Day jobs can be an excellent source of predictable income.

Side jobs are a good secondary source of income. Sometimes you will want an actual second job for a second employer with predictable hours, either long or short term. Picking up seasonal retail work around the winter holidays, for instance, can be rewarding, especially if you get an employee discount. My friend's husband worked at the Gap for the holidays when they were first married; everyone got clothes for Christmas that year!

But you should also look at monetizing something you are good at that other people need. Ideally, this is something you can do on your own schedule. Flexibility can be a big perk at certain points in your life—for instance, when you have young children at home.

My day job, for example, was conducting audits for the IRS, but my second job was doing people's tax returns. Most people dislike doing taxes and would pay someone else to do them if they could, and my background with the IRS made hiring me a no-brainer. As an auditor myself, I was always scrupulously honest, so people knew they could depend upon the correctness of their returns should they end up being audited, but I also believed in paying only what the law required. My deep knowledge of the tax code ensured that they would get the tax breaks they deserved. It was a win-win, and that extra money I brought in seasonally went straight to building up our investment portfolio.

Be productive and be paid for it. If you want a career in the arts, that's terrific, but get yourself a steady job so you don't have to starve in a garret. Even better, get that steady job, buy the house, and rent out the garret. Invest that stream of income and use the time you might have spent on a second job to pursue your art.

That, my friend, is what financial freedom can look like.

# Satisfy a Purpose

I have a purpose in everything I do. You do as well, but you may not have spent the time thinking it through and articulating it. I invite you to do so. Knowing your purpose gives you direction in life. A purpose can pull you forward when things get difficult.

My purpose in building wealth was not, as I might have originally thought, so that I could have the freedom to loaf around working on my tan. My purpose was twofold. First, I wanted to provide for my family. That purpose has driven many decisions. Sometimes it drove me to work late, or to buy life insurance, or once to quit a job that kept me from spending any time with my family at all. It helped me to decide in the moment what the best decision was for me, given that providing for my family was a core purpose for me. But I'll be honest, there was a second purpose behind my desire to build wealth: I never enjoyed being bossed around. I wanted the freedom to be independent, to be my own boss and choose my own direction.

The Pilgrims came to these shores with a singular purpose: to be free to live the way they chose. Our Founding Fathers declared their independence and Americans have fought and died for it again and again. We live in an amazing country. Our national character combines hard work with the rewards of a free-market system that supports individuals who are committed to making their own lives better and building stronger communities. Nowhere else on earth do you have this combination of daring, determination, and connection, and our free-market economy enables it all.

I believe we're all wired to want our own independence, to do things our own way. Taking charge of creating our own wealth means we are not a burden to others, not to our family or our community. One of my favorite authors is Ayn Rand, and I particularly love this quote:

> *Every man builds his world in his own image. He has the power to choose, but no power to escape the necessity of choice.*
>
> —Ayn Rand

I believe we each have the power to carve out our own life and create our own happiness. It is important—it is necessary—for us to spend time deciding what we really want, what our purpose in life really is. Otherwise, we're just behaving at random, making ill-considered decisions, choices that cancel each other out, or worse, ones that ultimately have the opposite effect of the values we hold dear.

Day-to-day decisions mount up. If they are aligned with your purpose, you will move forward toward your goals. If, however, they are not aligned, well . . . in my day, we used to refer to some folks as a "bump on a log." These were people who just did what they had to do to squeak by, rarely making their own decisions but instead following the crowd, taking the path of least resistance. But that path rarely leads anywhere. They didn't see that "going along to get along," not making any definite choices for their own lives, is itself a choice. It's a choice to have no goals, or to choose not to pursue them. It's just not a choice that leads to success.

In my experience, success and failure depend greatly on your mindset. Having a purpose makes it easier to see which choice is the right one, amid all the noise and uncertainty. It's a lens that ultimately makes your decision-making, and therefore your life, easier.

I also want to mention that—again, from my experience—I've found that you don't achieve wealth without sacrifice. Let's be honest: You don't achieve anything without some form of sacrifice. You may skip going out with your friends to get a good grade, or you stay late at work to put the final touches on a presentation. You get up early to get a run in to strengthen your cardiovascular system, or eat more steamed vegetables and less ice cream if your blood sugar trends high. We are constantly trading off immediate pleasure to reach a future goal.

Building financial freedom is no different. The more you can make it a habit, the less difficult it becomes. And reframing it as investing in your future or building your wealth, instead of thinking of it as depriving yourself now, can also make it easier to keep going.

It is always a joy for me when I meet people who have a similar mindset—they, like me, make their day-to-day decisions through the lens of purpose. Making choices that way seems less like sacrificing and more like building something that matters. This really is, for me, the joy of living.

## Establish Priorities

Purpose and priorities are inextricably linked. My priorities have always been taking care of my family and establishing financial independence for myself. In fact, I finally stopped working for other people only when my late wife, Bernice, asked me when I was going to stop making money for other people and start making it for us. It caught me off guard, but I quickly realized she was right: I had reached the point where it no longer made sense to trade my expertise and time for a paycheck. Again, my two priorities were completely aligned, and it made the decision to quit my day job remarkably easy.

I know a lot of people who have made different choices with their lives, largely because they had different priorities. I don't want to cast aspersions here; I like many of them, both friends and relations. My mother, father, brother, and I all had different points of view and different priorities, even though we were very close and had similar experiences. There are people out there who don't want to be land-lords; others who think being an investor is too difficult or mysterious for them. That's fine. This book is meant to show you many different paths to success. Problems arise when something detrimental to success actually becomes their number one priority.

For instance, I have trouble with gamblers. I know people who would rather gamble than invest their money. Do not conflate the two. Yes, there is risk investing in the stock market; anyone who tells you otherwise is after your money. But the level of risk from investing in a mutual fund, for instance (I'll get to those in a minute), is far different from putting your money on Lucky Number Seven at the roulette wheel.

I've seen friends lose money in casinos, at cards and dice, and at the racetrack. Sure, they have a lot of fun while they're gambling, especially when they're winning (surprisingly, when they lose, they don't want to talk about it!). But gambling can be addictive. I've known people to bet not only what they brought with them, which presumably they could afford to lose, but also exhausting their credit cards. Winnings are ultimately lost back to the house.

With stocks and bonds, you are putting your money into something that you and others are trying to build; with gambling, there is a built-in tilt toward losing. Remember, those beautiful casinos don't thrive on gamblers winning.

> *Gambling: the sure way of getting*
> *nothing for something.*
> —Wilson Mizner

Gambling often spills over into hobbies such as sports. If you're a fan, just keep in mind that the word is short for "fanatic." I don't want to take away from the fun of keeping up with a clean activity, especially if it's something that brings your family and friends together, but don't tell me you don't have time to research potential investment opportunities and then start quoting ten years of statistics for every member of your home team. And definitely don't complain that investing is too expensive after I've had to listen to you Monday-morning quarterbacking all year, thanks to your succession of season tickets and box seats.

This is where cleaning up your priorities can be useful. It's not "never go fishing" or "never do a crossword puzzle." It's keeping a check on those things that are consuming great chunks of your time while not moving you forward toward your goals.

Sometimes it's not so easy to recognize a problem. In the case of workaholics, you may think that you are spending your time wisely by building your career or making extra money—and those things can be true. But you have to look at the bigger picture. If you have a family, for example, where are they in the scheme of your priorities?

I have to admit to making this mistake myself. I spent two years managing a restaurant that I was in partnership with. To say that running a restaurant is all-consuming is an understatement. For two years, I rarely made it home before my kids were in bed. Most days, I left the house at six in the morning and didn't get home until nine at night. Finally, Bernice brought our three kids to the restaurant. She lined them up in front of me. "Take a good look," she told them. "That's your father."

What a wake-up call.

Yes, my priorities included taking care of my family, but that meant more than providing for them financially. Do you really want to sacrifice your relationships for money?

*All work and no play makes Jack a dull boy.*
—English proverb

Workaholism can narrow your vision. In addition to preventing you from developing friendships and professional relationships (which are a key factor in creating wealth, in addition to helping you live longer), a single-minded focus on work prevents you from growing in another arena. Just as I advocate for multiple streams of income, I also suggest having multiple areas that income can come from. In other words, not just going for the eight-unit apartment complex over the single-family rental home, but balancing real estate, say, with stocks or investing in a business. Workaholics tend to put all their emotional, physical, and mental eggs into one basket, while wealth is built on diverse streams of income and opportunity.

You won't be surprised to know that I told my partners they would have to find a new manager for the restaurant.

56

# Chapter Five

## Your Financial Milestones

Your journey to financial independence will be unique to you. There are, however, certain milestones that you will probably hit. The first one is financial self-sufficiency. Starting where you are now, do you make enough money to pay all your bills? If not, this is your first, urgent goal: What do you need to do to make that happen?

## Optimize Your Day Job

Your day job is your single biggest source of income. How can you optimize it? Are you in an industry that offers above-average pay?

According to the Bureau of Labor Statistics, an entry-level food worker makes an average of $13.76 per hour, which comes out to about $550 a week or $28,600 a year. There's not a lot of room for advancement either, unless you're in it to learn how to run your own restaurant someday.

Meanwhile, entry-level truck drivers make twice that, and the national average salary for experienced truck drivers is over $100,000. (And as my friend proved, you can turn even truck driving into an entrepreneurial opportunity if you have a compelling enough reason.) People who work in the field of computers make roughly twice the entry-level salary of registered nurses. And technology is reaching into every aspect of our lives more and more—meaning more and more opportunities abound.

I'm not saying you shouldn't do something you love and are good at, but I will say it makes your life a lot easier if your day job covers your bills. Can you find a way to use your strengths in a well-paying industry? What about working toward a promotion or even switching fields? It's never too late.

Among other careers, I've worked for the IRS as an auditor, I sold cars, I managed a restaurant, I oversaw loans in a bank . . . I have always had an eye out for ways to increase my value to employers, but also to maximize the amount I brought home from my day job. When something didn't work out, I moved on. Today, people call it reinventing themselves. I always saw it as doing work I was good at for people who valued me—and creating ways for them to value me even more.

## Case Study

Surveys show that half of all Americans don't have $1,000 in savings to cover an emergency expense. Say you borrow $1,000. If you go to a payday loan company, you usually need to repay that money in two weeks, with an additional $15 to $20 per $100 borrowed. That $1,000 today will cost $1,200 in two weeks. First, that's expensive! Second, if you are up against the wall to the point where you have to borrow $1,000 in the first place, what is the likelihood that you will have an extra $1,200 in two weeks to pay it all back?

If you don't, fees and interest continue to mount; that initial $1,000 becomes more and more expensive every day.

# Build Your Emergency Fund

Once you've got your needs met, your next milestone is putting together an emergency fund. This is a pool of money that is easily accessible for you to tap into when you need it. You can never predict what might happen: Your industry might take a hit; your employer might downsize or go bankrupt through no fault of yours; the whole country might shut down for a pandemic. The important thing is for you to have enough of an emergency fund that you can ride it out.

Smart people differ in their advice on how much you need in your emergency fund, but three months of living expenses is a good place to start. I'll come back to this later, when I talk about different ways to protect yourself from catastrophe.

The most important thing to remember is that it never makes sense for you to live paycheck-to-paycheck. Too many things can go wrong, and without a financial cushion, you have no good options.

Don't put yourself in a position where the money you need *costs too much*. What do I mean by that? If you don't have a financial cushion and something comes up, like your car breaks down or your roof needs to be fixed, you will need to do something to get money fast—which makes you vulnerable to predatory lending.

I'm not a fan of credit cards, unless you pay the entire balance every month, because they charge (as I write this) around 20 percent APR (annual percentage rate) as interest. But putting something on your credit card pales in comparison to predatory payday loans. The Better Business Bureau reports that some states allow payday loan companies to charge annual interest rates of *over 400 percent* (the highest reported was in Texas, at a whopping 652 percent APR).

Using these sources puts you at tremendous risk financially.

To make matters worse, an entire industry of scammers now targets people who use payday loan services. They buy (or hack) information from these companies and then criminally scam people by pretending to help them or loan them money just to get their banking and credit card information (which, of course, they then steal from), or by threatening them, making them believe they owe money from fraudulent fees or imaginary back payments.

These people are criminals trolling for easy victims. Needing money in a hurry makes you vulnerable. That is the opposite of financial freedom.

If your first milestone is to cover all your bills, your second is to build your emergency savings as quickly as possible. Get a temporary second job, have your cousin pay you to babysit or walk their dog, sell some stuff you don't need anymore. You are not looking for a long-term career here; you just want to beef up your savings so you're less vulnerable. Get that first $1,000 in place, then aim for three months' living expenses. This is money you will expect to use and replenish over time. I have even occasionally used it as working capital. Just be sure to replenish it as soon as possible. You will never regret having it handy.

## Build Your Investment Pool

You need money to make money. Whether you need money for a down payment on a rental property or to start investing in the stock market, or to buy into a franchise or start your own business, you are going to need ready money. Where is that going to come from?

Just as you may have had to hustle to build that emergency savings, you may have to keep hustling for a while to build up your investment funds, or what I like to call "working capital." Since this may be a more long-term project, I invite you to take some time to think it through. Flipping burgers on weekends for a few months while you build your emergency savings is one thing; you may not want to be stuck in that kitchen long term.

Extra income can come from many different sources:

- Bonuses and pay raises from your day job should immediately be shunted into your investment savings. If you don't see it in your checking account, you won't be tempted to spend it.

- Extra money can also be earned from a second, part-time job or from taking on overtime or other extra-paying project at your primary job.

- Seasonal jobs, such as working in retail during the winter holidays, can offer a double incentive: You can make extra money with no long-term commitment and use your employee discount to save on holiday gifts at the same time. These jobs are also easier to get because they need extra hands and aren't worried about keeping you on long term—although if you are a good fit, a temp job can sometimes turn into a longer-term second job. It's a good way to test the waters, for them and for you.

- Starting your own business on the side can be very rewarding. I used to do people's taxes, which kept me very busy for a few months of the year. If you are good at something like that, you can often charge more than you would make working for someone else while having the benefit of being able to work on your own schedule and in your own home. What competency do you have that others would pay for? People hate to do their own taxes, I can tell you that! Jobs like dog-walking may pay less, but you can walk several dogs at once, maximizing your time. See where you can either work for several clients simultaneously or provide a high-value, high-paying service.

- What assets do you already have that can provide income? Do you have a spare bedroom you can rent out? A lot of houses in Southern California, where I live, have small guesthouses in the back. If you have something like that, can you rent it to someone, either to live in or to use as their office?

- What do you know how to do well enough to teach? You could write an e-book on the subject, teach webinars, reach out to local groups to present for an honorarium (or to promote your book/webinar). The internet has made it possible to reach people around the world. What information do you have that's valuable enough that others will pay to learn it?

- Tap into your creativity. What can you make that others will buy? Again, sites like Etsy have made it possible for creators to connect with buyers around the country and the world.

- Where is free money just sitting, waiting for you? A lot of employers will match your contribution to a retirement account. In other words, if you have $100 taken out of your paycheck and put into a qualifying retirement account, your employer will add an extra $100, up to a certain annual amount. That's free money! In fact, if they match your contribution dollar-for-dollar, that is an immediate, 100 percent return on investment: Your $100 has just become $200, you didn't have to do anything, and there was zero risk involved. That's tough to beat . . . and yet, many of my own employees didn't take advantage of the plan. Don't leave money on the table. As an employer myself, I always wanted my employees to succeed financially. Check to see if your employer has any sort of employer-matched retirement plan available to you. Get educated about your specific plan. There may be a vesting period or other fine print. But when it works, it can double the funds you have available to invest in your retirement, and that is a boon, especially when you're just starting out. I was always happy when my employees took advantage of the program; I felt the ones who did were well on their way to building financial independence.

You are resourceful. Once you realize the value of making extra money—how you can make it work for you, how it can ultimately give you financial independence—you will find many ways to increase your investment funds.

> *When without resources, depend on resourcefulness.*
> —Sun Tzu

Another approach is to minimize what you spend. The more you can cut expenses, the more you will have to invest. Make a game of it! See how much fun you can have doing free things, like hiking, making your own delicious coffee, packing interesting lunches, going to street fairs to listen to music, picnicking in the park . . . .

All the while, your investment portfolio will continue to grow.

I have good news for you: You don't need a lot of money to get started. You want to start compounding interest (which I'll talk about later) and getting your money working for you as quickly as possible. In fact, no matter where you are financially, you can get started on building your wealth *today*. But first, we have to demystify some misunderstandings you probably have around money.

## Stay Productive

I love to multitask. I have never been satisfied doing only one thing or having only one job.

I always sought challenges at work, which helped me to earn more money through raises and promotions, and I always had something else that I was doing in my non-work hours to give me the funds I needed to invest in things like real estate and the stock market.

But I also focused on doing things I enjoyed and was good at. It makes it easier to sustain the effort if you enjoy the work you're doing.

# CHAPTER SIX

## WHAT WE GET WRONG ABOUT MONEY

We think that money gives us safety and happiness. Nothing could be further from the truth. Once we are beyond having our basic needs met (shelter, food, clothes), more money does NOT correlate to increased happiness. What makes us happy are actions like setting and meeting goals, doing things we're good at, and spending time with (and taking care of) people we love. If you stop thinking there's a dollar amount that will make you happy, you are going to be better able to create the wealth that will allow you the freedom to do the things and take the actions that will themselves increase your happiness.

Also, try not to be miserable along the way! Bernice and I had a great time building our wealth; we were a team, and we enjoyed the challenges and the successes every day.

So what are our actual options? If we're not using money to make us feel happy, what can we do with it?

## Money Can Sit There

You can sit on your money like a dragon on its golden hoard. This is essentially what you do when you stuff your money in a mattress—or, as is more likely today, in a low-interest savings account or (worse) a non-interest-bearing checking account. Yes, have some money that's within easy reach, but the bulk of your investment portfolio needs to be earning money for you. How does it do that?

## The Magic of Compound Interest

There are two kinds of interest: simple and compound.

With simple interest, you get the same amount every time. For instance, if you get 10% on $100 every year, you get exactly $10 every year. After ten years, you will have a total of $200.

With compound interest, the interest you earn becomes part of the principal; you earn interest on your interest. That same $100 investment at 10% compound interest would give you $10 in interest the first year, giving you a new principal balance of $110. The second year, you would get 10% of that balance, or $11, bringing the balance up to $121. The following year, 10% would equal $12.10, and so on.

At the end of ten years, your balance would be $259.37, almost $60 more—or 60% more in interest.

## Money Can Buy Things that Appreciate over Time

Have you ever bought a new car? If so, you are familiar with the concept of *depreciation*. When you drive that car home, it immediately begins to be worth less money. For one thing, it's no longer "new"—if you resell it or trade it in, you do so as a used car because, well, you have used it. People pay a premium for new; you, in fact, paid a premium to buy a car that had no prior owner. That vanishes the minute you drive off the lot.

And then, car parts start to wear out. Depending on how much you drive, how cold it is where you live, whether or not you've been in an accident, and dozens of other factors, your car is worth less and less every day. That is depreciation. But that's okay, because you bought it to get you from Point A to Point B reliably. With very few exceptions, people don't buy cars (or at least not the car they drive) in order to resell them for more money later.

The opposite of depreciation is *appreciation*. Not in the sense of gratitude, but in the sense of something being worth more, not less, over time. Gold is something people buy thinking that it will appreciate. Fine art is another. Coins, stamps, baseball cards, anything that goes under the heading of "collectible" is often purchased with an eye toward reselling it in the future for more than you paid.

In other words, you invested your money in an item that you believe will be worth more when you sell it. Your money is working for you by appreciating via this physical object. But it is never a sure thing—remember Tulip Mania! And, just as a quick side note, today people are buying and reselling digital collectibles as well. I don't know enough about how that works to comment on it, except to say that at least the ones left holding the bag of tulips in 1637 could plant their bulbs and enjoy some flowers. I don't know what you would do with your digital collectibles if you ended up with a (virtual) bucket of them.

> *Investing is laying out money now to get more money back in the future.*
> —Warren Buffett

Back to things money can buy that appreciate over time. Your house, if you're a homeowner, falls into this category. For most people, their home is their single biggest investment. Great! I'm a believer in real estate. I hope your home turns out to be a wonderful investment. However, the problem with your home or any other physical object you invest in is that it's difficult (not impossible, but difficult) to access the money you put into the investment if you need cash in a hurry.

Owning your own home (or another piece of real estate; more on that later) can be an important step toward building wealth, but it's not smart for any one thing to be your *only* step. I'm going to devote several pages to the idea of diversification, but for now, take it as a given that you shouldn't put all your eggs into one basket.

Finally, if you want to invest in collectibles, first of all, make sure that you have the space to store whatever it is so it won't get ruined; second, insure it to the hilt; and third—and maybe most important— never invest in something you don't understand. If you happen to be a wine connoisseur or an art critic and you truly understand the market, go for it. I know a gentleman who has a good side business buying and reselling vintage memorabilia, but he's not just a guy who goes to yard sales. He is an expert in a specific type and era who knows what sells, what doesn't, and who's buying. Don't think that if you buy up every comic book you see, you'll stumble across the first issue of *Superman*; that's a gamble you won't win. And you'll be tripping over boxes of comic books in your garage for years to come.

## Money Can Circulate

The third thing money can do is be lent out for a return on investment. This is what happens when you get a small business loan, for instance. Someone is giving you money so that you will have the capital to build a new business, which then earns money and builds the economy. This is not altruistic on their part—they expect you to pay them back the original loan along with interest.

The amount of interest depends on a lot of factors, including what interest rate has currently been set by the government (the Federal Reserve, or the Fed, sets short-term interest rates, which banks and other entities use as a benchmark) and how risky they think your business plan is. Banks and other lenders make money by charging you interest on the money you want to borrow from them. That amount is always more than it costs them to borrow money from the Fed.

The banks' best clients, the ones they feel are the least likely to default on a loan, get what's known as the prime rate, which is a little above the Fed's rate, but below what you can get elsewhere. This is a good reason to up your credit score: The less risky it is to lend you money, the less that money will cost you in terms of interest. Just like in your own investments, lenders expect to make more money when there is a higher risk that they might lose the money they shelled out.

The same principle can work for you. You can make money by lending your money to companies so they can grow their businesses and make more money. The return on your investment depends on a number of factors, including the global economy and how risky *their* business plan is.

How individuals lend corporations money is by buying shares of stock in their company.

# PART TWO

## GETTING IN THE GAME

# CHAPTER SEVEN

## GETTING STARTED IN THE STOCK MARKET

In my early twenties, I moved to Los Angeles and attended Los Angeles City College. I took an economics class, and I thought I would learn about the stock market. Imagine my shock when I learned that my college professor, the one who taught economics, did not know anything about the stock market. He himself had no stock investments at all.

This was the 1950s, and I was appalled. I never did learn anything about stocks in the classroom. Instead, I had a wonderful opportunity a little later at Los Angeles State College—but not in the classroom. I was able to join an investment club supervised by an accounting instructor. He had us start with a fictitious $1,000 investment. At the start of the class, each student selected their own portfolio. At the end of the semester, I ended up in the middle return on my paper $1,000. But the best lesson was that I got a close-up look at other people and how they invested. I was able to see why some students actually lost money while others did better than me. This was immensely useful.

The hands-on, no-risk experience revealed human nature and the types of decisions that drove the market. It was at this time I decided the kind of investor I was going to be. I wasn't going to "bet" heavily on new, unproven companies, and I also wasn't going to put everything in a T-bond (Treasury bond) and sit on my hands. I would be an active investor, and my focus would be on a combination of dividends and stock appreciation.

I kept it simple: I would aim for a 10 percent growth pattern. Ten percent would keep me satisfied.

Ten percent may sound high to you, but it's also the average annual stock market return over the last seventy-five years. Some years have been up, some have been down, but over time, it averages out to about a 10 percent gain.

I wasn't going to try to beat the stock market. I was perfectly satisfied with a middle-of-the-pack win.

This is where I take issue with people who see the stock market as gambling. Now, some people *love* to think of it as gambling. There's an emotional rush that some people get from thinking that they're risking everything on the roll of the dice. The problem is that it's a terrible way to approach the stock market. You're not in competition with it! It's not a winner-take-all, zero-sum-game. You are investing in the future of businesses, the underpinning of our economy. You are investing in *employers*, in companies that are building our economy, in growth. If you are looking at it as a game to "win," you are very likely to make terrible decisions, especially if the market is on the downswing—which it will be sooner or later.

By the same token, if you're convinced gambling is bad and that the stock market is a gamble, you risk missing out on a key way people can grow their money over the long term.

This is critical: You have to think of the stock market as a long-term investment. There are a couple of reasons for that.

The first is that buying and holding—not buying and selling and buying some more—is how to get closest to the average stock market return. Fees and taxes that come with churning your investments can eat into your gains if you are constantly selling and buying stocks. If you don't hold your investment long enough, you have to pay higher taxes on the money you earn from selling (as with any tax questions, I am not providing advice; talk to a tax professional and make sure you understand the tax implications of any decision you make).

The second reason is that trying to time the stock market is a fool's game. High-tech investors use computer programing with a coded formula to make logical steps to prompt a buy or sell decision . . . and they still can't time the market. Countless studies have shown that individual investors do better either investing as soon as they can financially or by dollar-cost averaging than by trying to time the market. I'm not saying don't sell a stock that you no longer believe in; of course you should do that, just as you should buy stocks because you think they're going places or because you want to diversify your portfolio. What I'm saying is don't be ruled by your emotions, whether it's the cockiness of having gotten something right or the panic of a bear market. Keep your emotions and your investments on an even keel.

## What Is Dollar-Cost Averaging?

Dollar-cost averaging is a fancy name for making investing a habit.

Instead of trying to time the market, you simply put the same amount into an investment at regular intervals. Weekly, every two weeks, monthly . . . whatever works for you.

Frequency does matter. Investing a smaller amount every couple of weeks spreads out the risk of trying to time the market.

Say you're investing $100 every week in a mutual fund. (This is not advice! Just an example.) If the fund's share price goes up, your $100 will buy fewer shares. If it goes down, you can buy more shares. Over time, market volatility evens out.

One Schwab study showed dollar-cost averaging netting almost as much as perfectly timing the market—and it's easier!

ROBERT BARBERA

# Find Mentors

After graduating from college, I joined the Internal Revenue Service. This was a fantastic learning opportunity for me. I was being paid to read hundreds of tax returns to see how investors were doing. I learned so much from this job.

I also made it a point to learn from people who knew what they were doing. When I was a kid, I caddied at the local country club. It became clear to me very quickly the social divide between the golfers and the caddies, and I knew which side of the chasm I wanted to be on.

Find people who are already successful, see what they're doing right, and learn from their mistakes.

> *Great leaders surround themselves*
> *with great mentors and advisors.*
> —Carol Sankar

The best part of this period, my early years with the IRS, came after I located a stockbroker's office in San Marino, California. Living out on the West Coast, we were three hours behind New York. The workday was already well underway back there by the time we got up in the morning. Several times a week I would go to the broker's office at 6 a.m. before starting my regular job at 8 a.m. Pacific time. I wanted to see what decisions wealthy investors were making that day; I wanted to listen to them talk about how they made their choices.

This daily dose of mentorship gave me, by far, my best education to broaden my understanding of the stock market. The investors I met in the stockbroker's office were friendly, enjoying the good days and ready to challenge the market after a bad day. I am forever grateful to have met people at the top of the income strata who were willing to let me learn from them. Sadly, the broker's office closed down when the internet became a more advantageous way to invest. There is a lot to be said for learning in community. I think we underestimate how important relationships are, and the willingness people often have in sharing their expertise and advice when given the opportunity. This is another great thing about America—how much people want to help one another up the ladder of success. There's a generosity of spirit that has allowed me to learn from those who went before me. I've tried to do the same; if someone asks how I succeeded in stocks or real estate or anything, I've always tried to be as transparent as possible, answering questions, showing them the ropes. These books are an outcropping of that deep desire to help as I was helped.

But I'll tell you something, just between you and me: Only one in ten of the people I've mentored was actually willing to do the work.

Years after my days hanging out at the broker's office, I would go to a coffee house for breakfast and listen to customers talk about life. They, too, were friendly, like the community at the stockbroker's place. But they were often complaining about whatever was going on in their lives, always victims of something. There was no positive energy there, no intention to take any action to improve their lot. It was a striking example of how different people approach life.

Once again, I knew which side of the chasm I wanted to be on.

# CHAPTER EIGHT

## WHAT TO DO WHEN (NOT IF) DISASTER STRIKES

I always tell my children, whatever you're doing, you always need to keep one foot on solid ground. Because the other foot is on a banana peel.

I'm not going to pretend that investing isn't risky. Of course it is. I always knew that something could go wrong, and often it did. That's life. The unexpected will happen to you, and sometimes it will be wonderful, while other times it will be terrible. It's not your fault. You have no control over that.

But you do have control over what you do, what safety net you create before you take a risk, and how you plan to meet your problems when they do show up.

> *Don't worry. It can be solved.*
> —John Barbera (my father)

You must plan for failure. You must assume everything will go wrong. And then you must have confidence that you can make it better.

# Worst-Case Scenarios

Can you take the loss? When we talk about risk tolerance, that's really what it comes down to. Are you going to be able to handle the consequences of failure?

If you think about it in the abstract, the immediate answer is probably no. We're human beings—we hate to fail! We think it's going to mean we're terrible or stupid or we don't know what we're doing. But remember, taking no risk at all means your money can never work for you, and that is its own kind of failure.

So, what to do?

Don't think about it in the abstract. Think about it concretely. If you took whatever action you were contemplating and it completely failed, what would you do? Don't ask this in any kind of existential way! Sit down and figure out, step by step, what you would do.

Here's an example. I spent a good portion of my adult life buying and selling apartment complexes. First, I looked for a good deal with a high potential for return, then I added to the mix that I wanted to be in certain neighborhoods, then I realized that I needed the buildings to be within a certain distance from each other so that my maintenance teams and I could easily manage the circuit of taking care of them. There was a lot of buying and upgrading by parlaying one property into something better.

And sometimes, things went wrong.

But I always had a backup plan. In fact, I usually had several backup plans: I had multiple streams of income so my family wasn't going to go hungry, and I had other investments I could liquidate if I absolutely had to have cash. Specifically, we could have sold our house. I loved my house, but at the end of the day, it was a piece of solid ground for my foot to stand on while I took risks with apartment buildings. We could have moved into one of our own apartments; my kids would still have had a roof over their heads. It never came to that, but I knew if it did, I still had options.

Never put yourself in a situation where you have no options.

This book is about financial wealth, but I believe in having options no matter what life may throw at you. For instance, you may think you have a secure income from your day job, but that can change. I've left several jobs, sometimes because I was done with it, once or twice because the job itself ceased to exist. Companies fold, your priorities change, new bosses come in and suddenly you find you just can't work there anymore. If that is your only source of income, you are just as at risk as I was when I emptied our savings, borrowed from my father and brother, and found myself with an eight-unit apartment building and quite literally $25 to my name, which had to last us until my next paycheck at the end of the month. It's a great story now, but at the time, it was a stretch.

And yet, I've never lost a bit of sleep. Isn't that amazing? With all the risks I've taken in my life, I've never lost sleep because I've always had a backup plan. If there had been an unexpected expense, I had plenty of options. I've already told you we were ready to sell our house if we had to and move into one of the apartments, but that wasn't even Plan B. I could have gone to my new tenants, for instance, and offered them a discount on their annual rent if they paid it upfront. I have friends who rented out their house and moved in with their in-laws for a year while they recovered from an industry-wide slowdown. Another acquaintance, an empty nester, rented out her daughter's room when a sudden expense threatened her ability to pay her mortgage.

If you're married, can you switch which one of you is home with the children while the other is in the workforce? I know a lot of families who've done that when the major breadwinner was out of work for a while. Bernice and I did something similar when we were first married; we didn't have children yet, but she worked full-time while I got my degree. Once I got a job at the IRS, she quit her job and we started a family. (I told her she'd never have to work another day. Ha! Again, I wasn't being dishonest, just naive. Bernice not only did a splendid job raising our children, but she was also my partner in our real estate endeavors and a very savvy businesswoman herself.)

There are always solutions, but it is infinitely better to figure out what they are—and do whatever you need to do to line them up—before you actually need them.

*When did Noah build the ark, Gladys?*
*Before the rain. Before the rain.*
—Nathan Muir (played by Robert Redford in *Spy Game*)

It's also useful for you to acknowledge the risks. It demystifies them. Do not shy away from potential danger. You will be better prepared to handle problems if you look at them squarely before they happen, and you will be more attuned to potential warning signs. Sticking your head in the sand will not keep you safe. Instead, dig deep. List everything that could possibly go wrong.

If you don't know what the risk is, you can't build your defenses or mitigate against it. Sure, sometimes you will be caught off guard; what went wrong will be something you could never have seen coming. But an emergency plan in place for one disaster can be finessed to cover a different calamity. It's when you naively (or arrogantly) think that nothing can go wrong that you are inviting trouble.

The line in the sand is clear: Do not take a risk that would leave you or your family destitute if it didn't work out. Always have a backup plan, have emergency savings, have plenty of insurance (including life insurance), build that safety net. And don't let greed or the fear of missing out (FOMO) blind you to the dangers inherent in any opportunity. Imagine that the worst happens: The startup fails, the charismatic broker turns out to be Bernie Madoff, your investment property burns down . . . what would you do?

No, really, what *exactly* would you do? Write down your disaster plan. Take stock of your assets now. List every possible thing you could do if something goes wrong to keep a roof over your head and food on the table. Get those emergency savings together. Let people know you're available to tutor their kids or walk their dogs, just so you temporarily have that extra trickle of income. If you don't need it, great! It goes into your working capital. But if you do, you'll be glad you have something in place that you can grow instead of needing to start from scratch.

# CHAPTER NINE

## DIVERSIFICATION IS THE BEST DEFENSE

This is probably the most important chapter in this book.

I really need you to understand that the difference between sleeping well at night and waking up in a cold sweat is knowing that if one investment or opportunity or job goes south, you have multiple other sources of income to shore you up in challenging times.

This may be a new way of thinking. As human beings, we value security. We like to have one answer, know it's the right answer, and be done with it. This is a very old-school approach—the idea, for instance, that you'll find one employer for whom you will work over your entire forty-year career, maybe getting the occasional promotion and bonus. Oh, and they will also pay you a pension, so you are in fact dependent upon them until the day you die. This idea of working for one company used to be the ideal. It represented lifetime security.

This is a fantasy.

If it ever worked that way, it doesn't anymore. And if it did magically appear, I urge you not to fall into the trap: Having only one source of income that you are going to depend on for your entire life exposes you to tremendous risk if something happens to that income source. In fact, this term "exposure" is used in stock investments as well. It's when your investment portfolio depends too heavily on one stock or one industry. If something were to happen to that industry, the bulk of your wealth could be wiped out. Remember my example of horse-drawn carriages? I rest my case.

It is crucial, then, that you diversify not just your streams of income, but also your investments themselves. We've talked about diversifying your income in terms of having a second job or side hustle, taking stock of your assets, and putting together a plan in case of emergency.

How can you do the same with your investments?

## Diversify Your Investments

The first thing we should talk about is asset allocation.

Let me take a second to say that not everyone agrees with diversifying your investment portfolio. Warren Buffett famously said, "Diversification may preserve wealth, but concentration builds wealth." He goes on to deride those who diversify as ignorant ("Diversification is a protection against ignorance"), implying that so long as you know what you're doing, you can put all your eggs in the one basket that is going to make your money grow the most.

I think that's a dangerous philosophy.

The more on-point quote by Buffett is "You only have to do a very few things in your life so long as you don't do too many things wrong." That is the most Monday-morning quarterbacking quote I've ever heard! I respect Mr. Buffett, but here I think the difference is clear: He is talking to a very few people who live and breathe the stock market, and who probably have vast amounts of resources should they do something "wrong" and their investment is wiped out.

Me, I'm talking to you.

You and I are not greedy. We don't need to beat the market. The stock market is by definition diversified; it contains around 2,400 different companies in every possible sector. And it has historically delivered about a 10 percent return over the long haul. Some years up, some years down, but we don't care because we are taking a long view of the matter.

*You must be diversified enough to survive bad
times or bad luck so that skill and good process
can have the chance to pay off over the long term.*
—Joel Grenblatt

Even Buffett agrees that diversification preserves wealth.

That's what we're after. We're not gambling. We are taking a long view. We are content with a return that is well above inflation, and we are going to diversify so that no one company or industry falling apart will leave us scrambling to find a part-time job when we're eighty.

*There are two kinds of forecasters: those who don't
know, and those who don't know they don't know.*
—John Kenneth Galbraith

No one has a crystal ball. No one knows what new disruption is going to make an entire industry superfluous. No one can anticipate bad actors like Kenneth Lay of Enron, who used entities to hide debt and overstated revenue with numbers pulled out of thin air; certainly, no one could anticipate that auditors at a well-known certified public accounting firm would look the other way.

Let's take it as a given that you should diversify. Here's a primer on asset allocation.

## Asset Allocation

Asset (or investment) allocation is a type of strategy whereby you put money into different types of assets. For instance, bonds tend to be more attractive when stocks are going down. Cash is great to have on hand in an emergency or when an opportunity for direct investment in a business or property arises. Think of it as different buckets and you'll put some of your money in each. Different buckets have different risks and different potential rewards.

The general term of *asset allocation* just refers to putting things in different buckets. What each bucket is and how much, percentage-wise, should be invested in each bucket are up for debate. There is no one right answer, but a lot of people have opinions.

Here's an old-school formula for allocating your investments. Please DO NOT look at this and blindly assume that just because it's old-school, or you may hear it repeatedly among financial advisors, that this is the perfect way to invest your money. I don't believe it is, but I do think it's a good starting point for a conversation about the different types of investments or "buckets" for your money to be divided into.

- Cash: 10%
- Bonds: 20%
- Stocks: 60%
- Precious Metals: 10%

That adds up to 100 percent of your investments.

This is a very traditional allocation. It's useful as a benchmark, but you should always adjust using your own situation. For instance, if you are just out of college and have a long investment horizon, you can afford to put more of your investment in stocks, which carry more risk but offer more reward, than someone who is on the verge of retirement. What do I mean by "afford"? If you are young and the market goes down, or even crashes, you can wait it out. You're not yet touching that money; you don't need it yet, so you can wait for the market to recover—and, historically, it always has. You have plenty of time for the market ups and downs to even out before you need to sell those assets to access that money.

This is not true as you near retirement. You are usually warned to be more cautious if you will need access to that money in three to five years—and by cautious, financial advisors usually mean taking it out of stocks and putting it into bonds, which tend to be more stable, if lackluster, or into cash equivalents.

In fact, there are many retirement accounts (or, if you have children, educational savings accounts) that offer investment funds tailored to your individual needs. These funds have targeted dates, either for when your child is headed for college and you'll use the money for tuition, or when you plan to retire and start using the money you've been saving. Over time, the accounts move your investment from assets that are riskier, or more heavily dependent on stocks, to a fund that relies more on bonds, which tend to be less risky. The idea is that, when you need the money, it is more likely to be available. You don't want a sudden dip in the stock market to coincide with you needing to withdraw that money to pay for your retirement or your kid's college. These kinds of targeted funds serve a need, particularly for people who feel uncomfortable making their own financial choices. The downside is that it takes the decision of how you want your money allocated out of your hands.

But you can learn from the idea. You will want to "balance" or "rebalance" your own investment portfolio over time, depending on a lot of variables. This means realigning your asset allocation to take the best advantage of the current economy, other opportunities you may have for your money, your own risk tolerance, and your financial goals.

Something we don't talk about enough is that it's not just the allocations that matter, but the quality of the stocks/bonds/etc. within the allocation that will make the biggest difference. I'll go into this more later, when I discuss what to look for in a stock before you decide to buy.

Even this traditional allocation, which has revered history behind it, should be approached with caution. Market behavior isn't beholden to tradition. At any given time, the market will favor one allocation over another. Holding all of them smooths out your risk, but you need an allocation that will suit your particular needs at any given time. For me, this traditional allocation is a bit stifling.

Let's look at each bucket.

## Cash

Cash is king. The first purpose of cash is to be readily available in case of emergency, to withstand economic downturns, or to help you take advantage of a new opportunity, all without disrupting your investment account. You don't ever want to be forced to sell a stock at a fire sale price because you don't have the cash to cover an emergency. In addition, having cash in your portfolio gives you the ability to quickly access opportunities, both in the market and out of it.

As I write this, the stock market in the U.S. is having one of its many volatile periods. I saw a headline the other day that was something along the lines of "Why Is the Stock Market Losing Its Mind?" And the reason usually involves remembering that the stock market isn't actually alive. It has no mind to lose. It is made up of human beings who sometimes react to events—or often not even to actual events, but only to the possibility or perception that something *might* happen—by panicking.

First, in the immortal words of Douglas Adams:

*Don't panic.*

Second, having cash as a part of your portfolio puts you in a position to never *have to* panic. There are all sorts of recommendations of how much of your portfolio should be in cash or "cash-equivalent" (which I'll get to in a minute). I mentioned above that the traditional advice is to keep 10 percent of your assets in cash. But to me, any number is arbitrary. It's not one-size-fits-all. Here are some things to think about:

- Do you have an emergency fund? If not, that needs to be your first order of business, as I mentioned earlier. Your emergency fund should have, at a minimum, three months' worth of living expenses. If you don't know what that looks like, take a step back and create a budget.

- To make a budget, start by writing down every penny you spend for the next month: rent or mortgage, car payments, phone bill, utilities, insurance, gas, groceries, entertainment, everything. Don't judge it, don't try to change it yet, just write it down. Add 10 percent because you probably missed something. Multiply it by three. This is the bare minimum you need in cash for your emergency fund.

- How many sources of income do you have? If you have a second job or a side hustle or a working spouse or passive income from another source, then probably three months is all you need as an emergency fund. Why? Because you are not relying on one single source of income and will therefore not be completely without income if you were, say, to get downsized in your current day job. As long as money continues to trickle in from another source—which you might want to beef up now, before you need it—then your emergency fund will last longer than three months. Ideally, you want to be able to stretch it out so that you can manage six months without your primary source of income.

- If your primary source of income is your *only* source of income, you need six months' worth of cash in your emergency fund. And I highly suggest you start thinking more flexibly now about what else you can do on the side to earn money. The way today's corporate economy works, you are highly exposed— to use Wall Street language—if you have only one source of income. Besides, money from a secondary source over and above what you need to live on can quickly add up to a good-size investment fund, giving you the opportunity to buy a rental property, for instance, or partner in an up-and-coming business, or create a stock market portfolio. In other words, it can become the money you need to build your future wealth.

- Once you have determined how much cash you need in your emergency account and have funded it, then you can make some decisions about how much cash you need for what I call "working capital." I'm not going to lie to you—I have often used my emergency fund as working capital. I believe cash buckets are meant to be used and then refilled. However, there is also value to creating a cash bucket that is meant specifically for investments. This is doubly true if you're looking to invest in something like real estate, where you will need significant money up front and at a specific time. Sure, stocks may offer you a greater return on your investment than a cash-equivalent investment, but you are at the mercy of the market if you need to cash out quickly. If the market is having a downswing just as you need to sell stocks for your goal investment—like, in my case, an apartment building—you may suddenly find yourself short. That is not where you ever want to be.

Do you see how saying something like "Ten percent of your portfolio should be cash" is meaningless? When you're starting out, 100 percent of your portfolio is probably cash: You're building your emergency fund, you're putting together your working capital, it's all cash. Then, as you start to invest, you'll add stocks and other assets, and the percentages will shift over time.

## What Is Cash-Equivalent?

Cash in hand always feels good. On the other hand, I don't suggest stuffing your mattress with twenties. That is not a smart way to keep wads of cash because cash in your mattress isn't working for you. It's not earning any interest. Keep some cash in tens and twenties in the house for emergencies—in a natural disaster, for instance, ATMs might go down and you might need some cash for gas or groceries—but at a bare minimum you want a good chunk of your cash to be earning interest in a savings account.

Your checking account is also cash-equivalent in that you're using it to pay bills directly these days, but it's probably not earning interest there. You want to keep that balance just above what you need to pay out every month, but as much as possible, you want to keep cash in something that earns interest.

A savings account, for interest, is a liquid account earning interest and makes great temporary storage for money you will use soon.

*Money does not buy you happiness, but lack of money certainly buys you misery.*
—Daniel Kahneman

Savings accounts are not the only possible temporary liquid accounts. While a little interest is better than none at all, more interest is, well, *more*. The important thing here is to understand the cost of increased interest (in other words, the return on your investment), because there is one, no matter what investment you're looking at.

The cost of a bigger return on investment is nearly always risk or access/time, or both.

What do I mean by risk?

Let's say your Uncle Arthur needs a loan to get his car fixed. He has not read any of my books and does not have an emergency fund, but he does have you. He asks you for a loan of $1,000 and offers to pay you back an extra $100 when he repays the loan in three months. In other words, you will recoup your entire investment plus 10 percent in only three months.

That's a great rate of return . . . if you get it.

No matter how nice a guy your Uncle Arthur might be, it is riskier to lend him money than it is to keep that money in your savings account. His car may break down again or he may have another emergency, or he may lose his job and be unable to repay you, either on time or at all. Lending him money carries more risk than lending your bank money, which is essentially what you are doing by opening a savings account and why they're willing to pay you interest in the first place. The rate of return is higher with your uncle because the risks are also higher.

But risk is not the only dimension someone is willing to pay for. I also mentioned access/time. A certificate of deposit (CD), for instance, has virtually no risk to you so long as it is FDIC-insured. So how can they offer a better interest rate/return on investment than the savings account at your local bank? Because when you buy a CD, you are giving up having *access* to that money for a certain amount of *time*. It is not always true, but it is often true, that the longer you are willing to let them hold onto your money, the higher the rate of return they offer. You are trading access to that money for a fixed length of time in exchange for a greater interest rate.

Risk and access/time are both components of every portfolio. It's not wrong to take a risk with your money, just as it's not wrong to tie your money up, sometimes for years. But it's important that you understand what price you are "paying" to get that better potential return. You can't make an informed decision unless you fully understand what you are giving up in exchange.

Now that we understand some of the factors behind different interest rates, let's take a look at some cash-equivalent securities. By definition, these are investment vehicles that can easily and quickly be converted into real cash-in-hand. They are generally low-risk and low-return, but any return is more than your piggy bank gives you. Reminder: This is a terrific asset class for money that you either know you will need relatively soon or that you may need in an emergency. We don't mind getting a low return on that kind of money because we are trading the lower return for a lower risk and easy access—exactly what we trade for higher returns, but in the opposite direction.

Cash-equivalent alternatives include:

- **Treasury Bills**

  T-bills are backed by the full security of the U.S. government and are considered the baseline for low risk. Here, you are lending the government money by buying T-bills. They are sold at a discount, and you get the face value at maturity. The interest is the difference between what you paid to buy the bill (which is determined at auction) and the face value. You get your investment back plus interest at maturity, and while you do have to pay federal taxes on the interest, you don't have to pay state or local taxes on it.

  As you can see, what you're trading here for interest is access: You get your investment back only after a certain amount of time (fifty-two weeks or less). You can sell your T-bill before it matures, but you need to go through a bank, broker, or dealer. If you will need that money before a year goes by, you can purchase T-bills for shorter amounts of time: four-, eight-, thirteen-, seventeen-, and twenty-six-week bills are also available. One nice feature is that you don't need a lot of money to get started: The minimum purchase is $100, and it goes up in $100 increments. Another way they have made T-bills available to your average American is by selling them direct online from the government. If you are interested in learning more about T-bills, you can find out more at treasurydirect.gov.

- **Certificates of Deposit**

Here, you're lending money to a bank instead of Uncle Sam. Again, what they are trading you for is time: You can purchase a CD for short and longer periods of time (a few months to a few years), and interest rates will vary wildly. It's worth shopping around to see which institutions have the best available rates for a length of time that makes sense to you. The downside of CDs is, again, access: Withdrawals before the end of your CD's term are usually expensive, with penalties and fees. The plus side is that if your CD is FDIC-insured, there is no risk to your principal up to $250,000, at the time I write this. BE SURE TO CHECK THAT YOUR CD IS FDIC-INSURED! Do not take anything for granted when it comes to the safety of your investments.

*A Word About CD Ladders:* Many experts will suggest that you create a CD "ladder" where you have CDs maturing every few months, and you keep rolling them over into new longer-term, higher-interest CDs. I understand why they suggest it; it keeps your money earning the most possible interest available at the lowest possible risk, while at the same time giving you access to a chunk of money every year or even every six months, depending on how many CDs you have. But for me, the downside is that it requires you to tie up a lot of money; those best rates often require a higher investment and a lack of access for as long as five years at a time. What if interest rates increase during those five years? You're usually locked into whatever rate you signed up for. And if you have a better opportunity for that money, some of it becomes available every year or six months, but the bulk of it doesn't. That's not really a cash equivalent in my eyes.

To be fair, there are some CDs that offer ways around these drawbacks. No-penalty CDs let you withdraw before the end of the term, for instance, and step-up CDs may include one or two rate increases, but these are exceptions rather than the rule. As with every investment, you must do your own due diligence. To sum up, CDs may be part of your investment strategy, but think long and hard about the real opportunity cost of building a ladder of them.

- **Money Market Accounts**

These are like savings accounts, but with higher interest rates. So what's the catch? Usually, it's the balance you have to maintain. If your balance dips below whatever the required minimum is, you could find yourself paying fees that wipe out any extra interest. You should also be careful that you're looking at a money market *account* and not a money market *fund*—those are two completely different things. I'm not going to suggest that one is better or worse, but I will point out that one (the money market *account*) is FDIC insured, whereas money market *funds* are not.

- **Money Market Funds**

To give some context to my explanation of money market funds, I want to point out something about cash equivalents. To my mind, cash equivalents should give you some return on investment (ROI) while at the same time should be both safe and liquid, meaning you can access that money almost on a dime. (Other people, however, have slightly different opinions.) Short-term investments such as bonds or CDs that mature in up to one year, for instance, may have a place in your investment strategy even if they're not technically the same as cash. They're not as liquid as your savings account, but they are still usually low risk and generally have a higher ROI.

Which brings us back to money market funds. These funds make short-term investments more liquid for you. They are mutual funds (which I will explain in more detail later) that themselves invest in cash equivalents, such as CDs and U.S. treasuries, as well as short-term corporate debt, short-term government securities, and short-term debt that's been guaranteed by banks. They are considered very low risk (although, as I mentioned under Money Market Accounts, above, they are not insured the same way money in your savings account is insured by the FDIC). You buy shares in the fund; they pay you dividends on your principal. You can recover your principal by selling your shares any time you want.

It's pretty straightforward, but there are, of course, drawbacks. In a volatile market, panicked investors may pull their money, forcing the fund to liquidate at a loss if it can't fulfill all the redemption requests. This has happened on a few occasions and can cause the loss of some of your principal. After this happened to the Reserve Primary Fund in 2008, new regulations were put in to increase fund stability, but there is always a risk. Right? That's why you decide for yourself. Don't just follow gurus blindly, not me or anyone else.

> *Take no one's word for anything, including*
> *mine—but trust your experience.*
> —James Baldwin

The biggest danger I see with any of these vehicles is overinvesting in them. They are meant to be a place to keep money for the short term, or to be one step above your savings account as a parking place for your emergency funds. Use common sense when thinking about where to put your cash. Do you need a go bag for a possible natural disaster? Keep cash in easy-to-spend denominations in the bag itself. Need a place to be able to access money for rent and groceries while you look for another job? Talk to your bank about how to maximize the return on your savings account. Know that you'll need to access working capital within the next year for a big investment? Examine your options when it comes to trading access to your money for higher interest rates. But remember that none of these are good options for funding your retirement thirty years from now. Sure, they're safe . . . but the opportunity cost is high.

This takes us to our next bucket: bonds.

# Bonds

I am happy to explain bonds to you. I'd also be happy for you to skip these next couple of pages and go straight to learning about stocks.

I believe the opportunity cost is too high to make bonds a good choice.

Obviously, there are other opinions. As mentioned above, conventional wisdom recommends keeping 20 percent of your assets in bonds. Some targeted funds will move an even greater percentage of your assets into bonds as you approach retirement. They are seen as less risky than stocks, although perhaps a better term would be "less volatile." Because there is always risk, it just looks different. In the case of bonds, one of the hard-to-see risks is that the return on investment will not keep up with inflation. Another is the very real risk of junk bonds.

Here's what a bond is: It is a loan. You are loaning money for a fixed amount of time to someone and they are paying you interest over the course of that time, returning your principal to you when the time is up, also known as the maturity date of the bond. This is why they are considered beneficial to your portfolio: You can (generally) rely on getting that fixed interest payment on a regular schedule. It is your money making money for you in the form of interest and in a predictable manner, which can be attractive. Conventional wisdom suggests that it also evens out the higher risk represented by investing in stocks, which is what they assume you are doing with a big chunk of your assets.

Historically, bonds have generally been a safe haven during those times when stock prices have been unpredictable. While you won't get more at maturity than you loaned out (namely, the face value of the bond), if you bought your bond at a high interest rate and interest rates fall, then other people might want to purchase your bond for more than its face value because they can make more in interest over the remaining term than they could otherwise. On the other hand, if interest rates rise after you've purchased the bond, you won't be able to sell out early and recoup your investment. You would have to discount the price of the bond, which we'll talk about again when we get into junk bonds.

> *A nickel ain't worth a dime anymore.*
> —Yogi Berra

I bring this up now so you can understand a key risk factor no one really talks about when they discuss bonds: needing your principal in a hurry. Short-term bonds are considered almost like cash, but bond terms can be up to ten years. It can be difficult to recoup your investment if you need your principal back before the maturity date, especially if the economy is doing well; people have other options for investing their cash. Unlike stocks, bonds do not increase in value either because of company growth or company appreciation; at maturity, you will be repaid exactly what you invested and no more. Meanwhile, inflation has continued to eat away at the face value of the bond—the money you receive back will be worth less than it was when you invested it. Yes, you will have received interest payments along the way, and those steady payments are the upside of lending someone your money for that length of time. Just make sure you run some real numbers and that the outcome is worth it for you and your specific situation.

Who are you loaning money to when you buy a bond? It may be the federal government, which is historically considered very low risk, meaning that it is highly likely that your principal will be fully repaid with all the promised interest. These loans are known collectively as Treasurys: They may be Treasury bonds, Treasury notes, Treasury bills, or Treasury Inflation-Protected Securities (TIPS), depending on many factors, including how long it takes for the bond to mature—in other words, when do you get your principal back in full? Because they are so safe, they generally provide the lowest interest rates. You get less money back for lending to the federal government because you are only trading time, not risk.

There are also municipal bonds (aka munis). These are loans you make to government entities like states or cities or counties. They are not quite as low risk as the federal government, so you should expect a slightly better interest rate, and they have another benefit, which is that the interest might be exempt from federal and/or state or local taxes. That can make them a little more attractive. But they still probably won't offer a very high return on investment.

Then there are corporate bonds. With those, you are lending money to a company for a fixed amount of time. How is that different from stocks? When you buy a stock, you are purchasing a piece of the company. Its value may go up or it may go down, so there is more uncertainty in terms of recouping your principal. But the length of time you continue to hold that stock, that small piece of ownership in the company, depends on you (short of the company going bankrupt, which can happen).

When you invest in a corporate bond, you are lending that company money. You do not own any part of the company, as you would if you bought shares of their stock. The amount of time you are lending them your principal is a fixed term; you cannot recoup your principal until that term is up, unless you sell them in the resale bond market, where you risk losing money, especially if interest rates have gone up since you purchased the bond. Sound confusing? It can be. But because corporations are not as stable as our federal and state governments, you should get a higher interest rate with corporate bonds because you are trading your money for *both* time and risk. That higher interest rate is the reward they offer for the added risk. Which takes us neatly to junk bonds.

## Junk Bonds

What is a junk bond? A junk bond means that the company issuing the bond may or may not be able to pay back the interest and principal down the road—and the lower the likelihood of you getting paid back, the higher the interest they need to offer to bring in investors.

There are several agencies, most notably Standard & Poor's, Moody's Investors Service, and Fitch Ratings, that will evaluate the creditworthiness of the companies issuing bonds and then rate the bonds. They each have their own ratings systems, so be sure you understand what their specific rating means. The higher-rated the bond, the less likely they believe it is to default. Junk bonds have the lowest ratings.

However, junk bonds are also called high-yield bonds, which sounds much more attractive, doesn't it? Remember my "lending to Uncle Arthur" scenario earlier, where you lend him money and he promises to pay a fantastic amount of interest in addition to paying you back in full? Depending on how reliable your Uncle Arthur is, you may get everything you were promised when you lent him the money, or you may get some of what was promised, or, sadly, you may get very little indeed. Forget interest—you may never see any of that money again. Your uncle, like an uncreditworthy company, must promise a high yield—because no one would ever lend them money without that large incentive—but that promise may or may not turn out to be empty.

The only difference between this scenario and a junk bond is that you probably know how reliable your uncle is from years of personal experience, and you can go into the transaction making an informed decision. Junk bonds, not so much.

Junk bonds are issued by companies that have poor credit ratings. The only way they can raise money by issuing bonds is to offer high interest rates to lure buyers to the table. Sometimes they make good on their promises; sometimes they don't. One of the issues these companies face is that, because of their poor credit rating, they have less access to borrowed cash, a higher burden of paying back those higher interest payments on the cash they can borrow, and a subsequent pinch in cash flow that can make them less able to take advantage of opportunities that come their way.

It's like when a person is strapped for cash: It's hard to be creative when you're trying to make rent and pay off a high-interest credit card at the same time. It saps your energy and gives you very little margin for error. (Which is only one of the many reasons I recommend either paying your credit card in full every month or cutting it up.) The point is, the same circumstances that create a potentially high return on investment for you—a company's inability to borrow funds easily—also create the very parameters that make it hard for the company to succeed, even with borrowed money. The money itself can become a burden as the interest on the debt can choke the company to death.

There is also an active, often volatile market in reselling junk bonds. This can be where greed can lead to one's downfall. You may be able to buy a high-yield bond at 50 percent off its face value, meaning that for $1,000 now, you will get $2,000 when the bond matures. What a return on investment, over and above the interest payments! Who wouldn't snap that up?

The person selling that bond at half off, that's who.

*In principle, junk bonds are basically useful, but they are used excessively and irrationally.*
—Maurice Allais

You must remember that the bond is only for sale at that discounted price because the person who owns it now is so afraid of the company going under that they are willing to lose half of their principal just to get something back while the getting is good. Some investors are more likely to buy junk bonds when the economy is improving after a downturn, with the idea that a rising tide lifts all ships. Me, I wouldn't count on it. A rising tide doesn't help when the boat itself is leaking.

To be fair, non-junk corporate bonds are for the most part thought of as a secure investment. They pay a steady stream of interest, usually annually, and they hold first priority of company assets—which means that if the company does go bankrupt, bondholders get precedence over stockholders to pry their money out of the company coffers. That said, in bankruptcy, even the sale of a company's assets may not cover the bondholders' investments. You must do your due diligence in buying bonds just as you would in buying stocks.

I have only bought bonds one time, and I had no choice in the matter. As an employee of the Internal Revenue Service, I was pressured by a supervisor to buy U.S. Treasury bonds at a lower interest rate than my money was earning in a savings and loan. In other words, buying that government bond would immediately be a net loss for me, since that money would now be earning less than it could have. When I objected, my supervisor told me the IRS Los Angeles district director wanted all employees to buy bonds. He recommended that I not be the only one left in a district of 600 employees to refuse the director's "suggestion." Then he gave me some great advice: He told me to buy the bond and redeem it the next month. Which I did. And I've never bought another bond since.

> *Fixed-income investors worldwide—*
> *whether pension funds, insurance compa-*
> *nies, or retirees—face a bleak future.*
> —Warren Buffett

I have seen too many problems with bonds over the years to recommend them to anyone. My neighbor went all-in with bonds in her trust account. By the time she passed away, inflation had eaten into her investment so much that the face value of the bonds had only a 50 percent purchasing power for her heirs. A friend of mine purchased junk bonds at a 50 percent discount—and a heavy commission. When she wanted to sell them, they were being sold at a *75 percent discount*, a loss of half of her investment. A Beverly Hills insurance company that shall remain nameless purchased junk bonds that failed miserably, causing disruption for people who held insurance policies.

In my opinion, bonds are a menace.

## Precious Metals

Investing in gold or silver has helped people withstand paper currency fluctuations over centuries. Gold, if you'll pardon the pun, is the gold standard of precious metals; it is valued internationally and has a long history as a medium of exchange, keeping up with the many changes in how human beings develop their economies.

There have been times when both gold and silver made very good investments. Gold, for instance, increased from $272.65/troy ounce at the end of 2000 to an astonishing $1,895.10/ounce at the end of

2020, according to Macrotrends.net. Four years later, it's up another $600/ounce as I write this, far outpacing inflation. Silver also went up, from $4.58/ounce at the end of 2020 to $27.93 today, a 600 percent gain in value in less than twenty-five years. There are entire businesses devoted to buying people's old jewelry just for its value in raw metals.

So why should (or shouldn't) you want gold?

The first thing to understand is that you can't just pop into a store and buy a pound of gold. Gold *is* available for purchase: gold jewelry, gold coins, and gold bars. You can buy those from dealers and mints and online stores; you can get gold new or used, fashioned, refashioned, with or without a warranty worth the paper it's printed on.

Purity is incredibly important. "Investment grade" purity is at least 99.5 percent pure gold for gold bars, roughly the equivalent of 24K for jewelry. You have to trust the entity you're buying it from, whether that's a mint for coins or a dealer for bars or a jeweler for a necklace. And by "trust," I mean look into their business, see what professional organizations they belong to, get someone else to appraise an early purchase to make sure you're getting what you paid for.

Add to that the fact that gold coins and gold jewelry are also considered "collectibles." That means there is an additional premium on them that you wouldn't have to pay when buying pure gold. Of course, you hope they remain collectibles when you're ready to sell them, but the collectibles market is a fickle thing.

Finally, many gold coins and jewelry include other metals to make them stronger or change their color, which may or may not have an impact on their value.

There is also the question of storage. Where are you going to keep your gold? How will you insure it? How will you protect it? There are a lot of moving parts with something as portable and untraceable as gold.

Earlier in the book, I promised you a cautionary tale. Voilà—here's what *not* to do:

There was a lot happening with gold under President Nixon in the early 1970s; I will leave it to historians and economists to give you the fuller picture. But one of the repercussions was that it became legal for individuals to once again own gold in the U.S. I bought $3,000 worth of gold coins for about $35/ounce. Did I insure the gold or store it in a bank vault? I did not. Instead, I hid the gold in my house.

You know where this story is going.

Twenty years later, when I was moving, I went to get the gold coins. They were missing. I never did find them, and that was the end of my personal interest in gold.

But having someone else protect my gold in their safe would not necessarily have had a better outcome. Years later, when I was auditing gold dealers for the Department of Corporation, I came across a gold dealer who sold gold to clients and, for a fee, stored the gold in their own vault. Yes, that protected the gold from a home burglary or a fire, but what it didn't do was protect the gold from the dealer. The dealer resold the same gold to a different client.

Gold makes people do strange things.

Gold seems like it would be a great idea, but while the price has certainly increased dramatically, it is still difficult to translate gold into cash when you need it. You rarely can sell your gold directly to another investor, and dealers, as middlemen, can take a big cut. Coins, bars, and jewelry are inconvenient and potentially expensive to insure, store, and transport. It may be fun to own gold as a novelty but using it as a monetary exchange is tricky at best.

You can also invest in gold by buying stock in a gold mining company, for instance. There are even gold-invested mutual funds to take away some of the risk. But I don't think that's what folks mean when they suggest investing in precious metals. I think they mean real, physical metals—gold stocks are still stocks. And I'm not really sold on the idea that having physical gold bars lying around is going to save you in a stock market crash. Yes, they tend to go down less than the market during bear cycles, but that doesn't mean gold isn't volatile; it's just volatile in a different way and for different reasons than the stock market as a whole. Finally, it has yet to outpace the S&P 500 in terms of overall growth. If you had invested the same amount in an index fund five years ago, your portfolio would be worth around 30 percent more than your gold.

This, finally, takes us to the last (and generally largest) bucket for your assets: stocks.

# CHAPTER TEN

## STOCKS

I love participating in the stock market. I've always loved it. I love feeling that I am part of something very big, that I can participate in the American economy no matter how small my initial investment might have been. I love going to the store and buying a new Gillette razor blade, because by owning their stock, I own a little piece of Gillette, and buying that blade means supporting my company. I am a part of something bigger because of being in the stock market. That has always made me proud.

> *Although it's easy to forget sometimes,*
> *a share is not a lottery ticket ... It's*
> *part-ownership of a business.*
> —Peter Lynch

When we buy stock in a company, it's as if we are casting a vote for the success of that company. And many of these companies provide for our needs and those of our neighbors and fellow Americans: transportation, food, housing, medicine . . . they are all represented on the stock market. We can vote for companies we believe are doing good in the world, according to our own personal values. And if something changes, we can sell our stock and shift our money to back a different company, one more in line with our vision of ourselves and the world. That is freedom! It's also a relief: We don't have to make the perfect choice with every stock purchase. We can simply do the best we can, because we know we have the right to make a better selection down the road.

Here's the story of my first stock purchase. It was 1953; I was twenty-one years old and had always lived in New York. I had graduated high school and gone straight to work, and the company I was working for transferred me to Charlotte, North Carolina. One day on my way to work, I noticed a sign in a window promoting a 5.5 percent return. I thought, wow; my bank is only giving me 3 percent on my savings account—this is nearly double. I may have been young, but I could do the math. I went inside, a nice man met with me, and I signed over pretty much my entire savings account to him, about $1,000.

Let me be straight with you: I had no idea what I was doing.

This could have gone very badly for me. I thought I was signing up for a new savings account. A month went by and I started getting statements—not bank statements, but statements from the Canadian Railroad . . . which is when I realized I hadn't opened a savings account. I had bought stock. Not only didn't I know anything about the Canadian Railroad, but I also didn't know anything about stocks! Now, instead of interest, I was getting dividends, and I had no idea what they were.

I got lucky, not only that the gentleman didn't take advantage of my obvious ignorance, but also that I stumbled into the stock market this way. My parents had never invested in the stock market, and I knew nothing about it, but because I was now a shareholder, I became curious. It was the beginning of a lifetime of learning how stocks work.

There is a lot to unpack in discussing the stock market. The important thing to remember is that if you have too much of any one thing—for example, if any one industry, an individual stock, or a type of stock makes up too much of your portfolio—you are exposed to something going wrong in that one market.

For instance, stocks in a certain category sometimes create tremendous excitement, which pushes the stock price up. So far, so good. But the risk there is that people become desperate to invest in it, no longer looking at fundamentals but instead projecting their hopes and wild expectations onto the sector. This blind frenzy pushes stocks higher and higher—far beyond a true reflection of the value of the companies involved.

Sooner or later, stock prices can't go up anymore; savvy investors and even not-so-savvy ones can no longer justify the cost of the stock. This is called a bubble, and when it bursts, stocks don't just go down, they crater. We saw that in the Dotcom Bubble, which burst in 2000. This is why it's so dangerous to invest in only one sector. When you spread your investments out over different kinds of stocks, you don't eliminate all risk, but you do mitigate it. Go back and reread the section on diversification (Diversify Your Investments) if you need a refresher.

## The Value of a Stock Portfolio

Whether the stock market has gone up or down, in the long run it has been my experience to see the market always end up higher. Sooner or later. And that is the secret to the stock market: time. I will hammer this again and again: The value of a stock portfolio isn't in picking "winners"; it's in taking advantage of a long time horizon to give solid, dependable stocks time to appreciate. Being actively involved in your portfolio is not the same as constantly buying and selling. It's being watchful, looking for opportunities, moving out of positions that are underperforming or perhaps facing what you believe will be an insurmountable challenge. It's about staying vigilant, not playing the ponies.

My own average growth in terms of my portfolio has been very much like the growth in the averages below, which show what the long-range stock indexes have averaged over the ten years ending 12/23/23 (per OfDollarsAndData.com):

- S&P 500: 11.13% growth (13.19% if you reinvested dividends)
- U.S. Stock Market: 13.51% growth
- Russell 3000: 11.84% (per YCharts.com)

That's pretty solid growth. It's well above inflation. It's why you don't have to beat the stock market—if you simply mirror it, your wealth will increase dramatically *over time*. This is why you should start investing as soon as possible. Time is your friend.

There are several reasons why the stock market works so well to build wealth. First, the stock itself can appreciate. A stock's appreciation is the difference between the price you paid to purchase each share and the market price that a share is currently selling for. Pretty simple, right? Of course, not every stock goes up. Not every company succeeds. What makes one stock increase in value when another does not?

- The demand for and sales of a product or service increase.

- There's a favorable acquisition or merger.

- They've reduced production costs, potentially increasing profit.

- Their reputation has grown, sometimes justifiably, sometimes from hype from a variety of sources.

- The bottom line looks good: The company is showing increased profits or dividends.

One of the key things to understand is that as you are growing your wealth, the increase in the stock price is not taxable. It may be taxable as capital gains taxes, which tend to be taxed at a different (currently more favorable) rate than regular income. But that only kicks in when you sell the stock. Until then, you don't have to worry about it. Dividends and interest, depending on your investment, may be taxed.

I'm not trying to be vague here—it's that there are a lot of possibilities. I should know, having worked for many years as an auditor for the IRS. Which is why you should listen when I tell you to always, always consult a tax professional when it comes to the nitty-gritty of your personal situation and the tax implications of your investments.

## How Long Should You Hold Your Stock?

That depends. There are tax implications for holding something long-term versus short-term. Professional advice for your particular situation is always the way to go! For me, the length of time I keep a stock depends on a number of circumstances. I lean toward selling a stock:

- If there is no growth. We all make mistakes; there is no perfect way to evaluate a surefire winner. If I discover that a stock I chose is stagnating, then the money invested in that stock is doing nothing for me. I am losing the opportunity to put it into a stock that will grow. When that happens, I don't beat myself up about it. I simply sell and reposition.

- If the company promotes values that I don't believe in. There are plenty of fish in the sea. I don't have to put money into a company that doesn't hold my values. And neither do you.

- If competitors in the same business are moving ahead faster. I don't want the also-ran—especially if they end up being run out of business.

I put a lot of effort into deciding which stocks to buy. I credit the after-class investment club in college—which was a lot of fun, by the way. We compared notes, we kidded each other, we learned from each other. It's another thing I love about this country: how community coalesces around a project, a chance to learn and do something together. For nine months, we explored the market together. I traded on paper; no money changed hands. But I tried and I researched and I learned. At the end of the school year, my portfolio gains were right down the middle of the group at about 10 percent. What I learned there, I have come back to again and again, with actual money.

Some questions to answer before you invest in a company include:

- Have you conducted thorough research? Have you done your homework, followed a stock on paper, learned about the industry (either because you work in it yourself or grew up in it, or dove in with an open mind and a commitment to learning)? If so, you're in good shape to make an investment in a particular stock and/or sector.

- Is there an understandable trend pushing that company's products upward? Not a fad, not some bandwagon to jump on, but something that you understand and can explain to a child without using jargon? The world evolves. Something like a smartphone is clearly useful and has the potential to grow even more so; that is an understandable trend. Something like a new fad doll is not.

- Is the company evolving? Have they discovered or developed new resources to increase sales? Are they getting better and better at whatever product or service they deliver, and is that product or service becoming central to people's lives?

- Is a profitable takeover on the horizon? Will there be value added when there's a merger? Could a new partnership signal a growth phase for the company and their stock?

These are some of the key things that make me look at a stock as a potential purchase in the first place. I also look at them to make sure I'm well-diversified. I will want to buy a kind of stock I don't already own a lot of, for example, rather than go all in on one company or industry. I'll be talking more about diversification as we go on.

Stocks vary in all sorts of ways: the size of the company, the industry, how long they've been around. One way they differ, and it's one of the fundamental ways that stocks earn you money (as I learned from the Canadian Railroad), is dividends.

## Dividends

What is a dividend and how does it work? A dividend is a share of the company's profits that is given to an investor (aka a stockholder).

The dollar amount of the dividend is calculated per share. It's usually distributed quarterly. Different stocks pay on different dates; it's not like all your dividend payments will appear on the last day of the quarter, for instance. You can see what dividends you've been paid by looking at your account statement from your broker.

Dividends are also calculated as an annual percentage yield, meaning you can see how much your dollar investment in a stock will yield in dividends over the course of one year. Not all stocks offer dividends, and dividend yields vary widely—not just from stock to stock, but potentially from year to year, depending on how well the company is performing.

Early in your investing career, you are probably more interested in building wealth than in generating income. You have a long horizon for the stock market to go down and up and down and up again. This means you can be a little more aggressive with stocks that might have more risk to them (although you still want to diversify). Later in life, you might want your hard-earned investments to provide some reliable extra income. But in both cases, prioritizing stocks that pay shareholders dividends is a smart strategy.

When you're young and building wealth, you can automatically reinvest your dividends—it may literally be a box to click wherever your account is held (I am assuming these days that you have online access to your broker, whoever that might be). When you do that, what happens when a company pays dividends is that the money is automatically used to buy more shares of that same company, rather than being held as cash for you by your broker. Assuming it's a company you continue to believe in, reinvesting dividends in this way is a passive (as in it takes no work on your part and no "timing" of the market) approach to building your portfolio. Dividends are reinvested, turning into shares of stocks that then increase your dividends next time, which then purchases more stocks, which once again increases your holdings . . . you can see how this becomes a virtuous cycle. Just like compound interest provides a dramatically better return than simple interest, reinvesting your dividends can create a dramatic difference in your portfolio over time.

Time is your great friend when investing.

*Time is the most important ingredient in
any financial wealth-building strategy.*
—Suze Orman

Different stocks offer different amounts of dividends, paid on different schedules. Most often, they are paid quarterly. It's not a gift—it's the company sharing some of their profits with the people who are funding their growth. That would be you, the investor.

Not all stocks offer dividends. Why not? There are many reasons, but often it has to do with where the company is in its development. Younger companies, for instance, may still be investing in themselves. Stockholders primarily buy shares in companies they believe will grow and whose per-share stock price they believe will increase substantially. In those cases, it makes a lot of sense for a company to hold onto their cash and use it to continue to build the company, offering shareholders value in the increased stock prices and continued growth of the company's fundamentals.

Other companies simply prefer to offer returns in terms of the stock's growth itself. Famously, Berkshire Hathaway doesn't pay dividends because Warren Buffett believes it's better for his company (and his shareholders) to plow as much money as possible back into the company. He believes the greatest value he can offer shareholders is using the money he would otherwise dole out as dividends to create new products that will increase the value of the company. It's a strategy that works for him and appeals to the investors who buy his stock.

There are even different kinds of dividends: cash dividends, which can be reinvested or transferred to your brokerage account or your bank; stock dividends, which are issued in lieu of cash, allowing the company to reward shareholders while at the same time conserving their cash (although this also results in diluting the share price, since there are now more shares in circulation); and preferred dividends, which are paid to shareholders of preferred stocks. There are even more: property dividends, special dividends, interim dividends, liquidation dividends, final dividends. And since dividends are given out as a percentage of the share price, they increase as the stock's price rises.

Dividends are very attractive, but despite all of this, they are not the be-all, end-all when it comes to choosing stocks. They are just one factor to look at.

I have always preferred to prioritize companies that pay cash dividends. What can I say—I like the flow of money coming to me. I like that it's predictable. I like reinvesting it. Sometimes I like having it as cash on hand when I am interested in putting a deal through in real estate or some other opportunity. However, when I say that I want a 10 percent return on my investment, that is not in dividends alone. It can't possibly be. As I write this in August 2024, the top-five dividend-paying stocks in the Dow Jones Industrial Average are:

- Verizon Communications, with an annual dividend yield of 6.75 percent

- Dow, Inc. (the global chemicals producer, not to be confused with the Dow Jones), with an annual dividend yield of 5.19 percent

- Chevron, with an annual dividend yield of 4.69 percent

- IBM, with an annual dividend yield of 3.46 percent

- Cisco Systems, with an annual dividend yield of 3.28 percent

That's it. Of the thirty stocks tracked by the Dow Jones, only five have dividends of 3.28 percent annually or above. The entire New York Stock Exchange, which is composed of over 2,300 listed companies, lists only *fifty* stocks currently paying an annual dividend yield of 3.28 percent or more. Meanwhile, the current rate for a twenty-year

Treasury bond is 4.625 percent. Both are over the current rate of inflation, which was 2.9 percent in July 2024, although the Treasury bond clearly pays a higher interest rate.

If the Treasury bond is virtually risk-free, why would I suggest you overlook it in favor of stocks, the vast majority of which offer dividends far below inflation and come with risk baked in?

Because a Treasury bond will never increase in value, that's why.

If you hold a Treasury bond until maturity, you will be paid the interest on the bond, sure, but you will only ever get back at the end the exact same amount, or principal, you used to buy the bond. Your money is not reinvested; there is no opportunity for compound interest or growth. Sure, a twenty-year Treasury bond pays interest at a higher rate than most stocks pay dividends, but that bond is only ever going to be worth $1,000 at maturity, twenty years from now. That is not true of stocks.

Stock share prices have historically gone up, whether you reinvest your dividends or take them in cash. The underlying value of your investment increases as the company grows. Yes, there is a risk. Some companies underperform. Some even go bankrupt. There will be losers in your portfolio. But that is where diversification comes in. You have not put all your eggs in one basket, so you are not scrambled, if you'll pardon the pun, if one stock goes south.

Dividends can be an important consideration when choosing at least some of your investments, but they are not the only aspect of a stock to consider. If the share price is not poised to go up—that is, if other people don't continue to believe that the company is growing and has the potential to keep growing—dividends should not induce you to buy the stock. Again, they are only one piece of the puzzle.

A final note before we move on: As always, you should contact your tax professional to discuss how different approaches might have an impact on your taxes. Dividends, interest, and capital gains from selling shares all have some effect on your tax liability, and the one thing all government bonds bring to the table that stocks don't is the possibility that some of the interest earned might be federal, state, or local tax-free, or some combination of the above. What works for my situation won't necessarily work for yours, so get help from someone who knows their way around your individual tax situation.

# What Is the Dow Jones?

The Dow Jones Industrial Average is a benchmark index that tracks thirty large companies and how well they're doing. When they say the Dow is up, they mean the value of the shares of just these thirty companies has, in aggregate, gained value. Ditto if the Dow is down: These companies, together, have lost stock value.

It was created by Charles Dow in the late 1800s and named for him and statistician Edward Jones. The idea was that it would serve as a proxy for how the stock market was doing as a whole.

There are other indexes: The S&P 500 tracks 500 large companies, while the Russell 3000 tracks (you guessed it) 3,000 publicly held companies. Every index has its own strategy for coming up with its number, and there is no perfect proxy for the market. But for better or for worse, people tend to use the Dow as the benchmark for how well the economy is doing.

## A Word of Warning

One last thing before we get to the nuts and bolts of what I look for in a stock: You're going to make mistakes. You're going to put your money behind companies that underperform, or maybe even fail. Stock prices will go down. You will not hit a home run every time. And that's okay.

*Success isn't permanent and failure isn't fatal.*
—Mike Ditka

If a particular stock in your portfolio is not meeting expectations in growth or dividends or both, do something about it. Take action. Sometimes we hold onto a stock because we fear missing out when (if) it goes back up, but more often we're swayed by a sense of loyalty. There's an interesting psychological study that has shown people are unwilling to give up something they already have, even if they didn't value it highly before they got it. The study has been replicated a bunch of times, but this is pretty typical.

People were shown a mug and asked how much they would pay for it. Let's say they answered $10. They were then given that mug, and moments later were asked if they would sell it (or, in some versions, trade it) for something of the same value. Most people said no. In fact, most people weren't willing to sell their mug until the price offered was *twice* what they initially said it was worth.

Even if they hadn't valued it highly before they got it.

Even if they'd only owned it for a few minutes.

This is called the endowment effect, and it can wreak havoc with your portfolio. The name was coined by an economist, Richard Thaler, who went on to win the Nobel Prize. He also pinpointed the danger of the endowment effect on an economic level, which is twofold. First, it creates inertia in our decisions. We want to hang onto what we have, and that makes us reluctant to look into alternatives and slow to make a choice. Now, I don't suggest leaping before you look (in fact, I'll talk about that a little later), but there's a difference between taking a moment to prudently examine a situation and refusing to act because you don't want to look too closely at a stock precisely because you already own it.

The second danger he noted is underappreciating the opportunity costs of letting money sit someplace where it's not doing you any good, whether that's a mug you don't need that someone's willing to give you ten bucks for or a stock that isn't moving you toward your financial goals.

The good news is that once you understand the endowment effect, you can start to shake it off. One way is to pretend that you don't own it. Take a look at the fundamentals, which is our next section, with fresh eyes. If you had $1,000 to invest today, would you use it to buy that stock? Why or why not? Reality checks like this one can help you realize if you are hanging onto the stock because you truly believe it has the potential to grow, or if you are clinging to it only because it's yours.

There's no shame in having this knee-jerk reaction—one that scientists have discovered great apes are as prone to as humans, by the way. Just don't let it dictate your financial decisions. Don't be an ape! Use your noodle and recognize that loyalty to a company (or stubbornly holding onto a decision you previously made) is not a profitable business decision. It should never come at the expense of your future or your family's well-being.

# Chapter Eleven

## Fundamentals

Do not skip this section. This is where the rubber meets the road. One of the biggest mistakes you could make would be not doing your homework before you invest in a company. You are not throwing darts at the *Wall Street Journal* to decide how to invest your life's savings! If you want to have success at building wealth, you need to be willing to learn the language of business. You need to be able to understand a company's fundamentals and recognize whether or not it is likely to succeed, and you need to do it before you buy.

> *An investment in knowledge always*
> *pays the best interest.*
> —Benjamin Franklin

You can find much of this information in the company's prospectus. I like to say there's no place to hide in a prospectus. Don't be dissuaded by the number of pages (a lot) and the size of the typeface (pretty small). It can be a treasure trove of information.

Nowadays, you can also find a lot of information online, but be careful. A prospectus is a legal document, and there are consequences for lying or failing to disclose information. By contrast, much of what's online or in news stories is hype. I'm not saying PR people are necessarily lying, but they're definitely putting their best foot forward. There's a reason it's called "spin."

You can find a company's prospectus by going to the SEC's official website (at SEC.gov) and clicking on "Search Filings," then choosing "Full Text Search." You enter in the company's name or its ticker symbol, and then under the "Filing category" option, choose "Registration statements and prospectuses." Voilà!—it's like magic. Everything you need is at your fingertips.

I have developed my own strategy for deciding which companies were worth my investment. THIS IS NOT TO BE CONSIDERED FINANCIAL ADVICE. I am not a financial advisor. I make no claims to know what the right move for you, in your situation, might be. If there were a foolproof way of making money in the stock market, everyone would be a millionaire. There is no magic formula. And everyone makes mistakes, myself included. In fact, I'm going to start by telling you a story from my own life of exactly how NOT to pick a stock.

Many years ago, my neighbor, who was a banker, came to me one day and said, "Robert, I've got a tip for you. A guy came into the bank, and he was talking about a mining stock in Canada. They have gold and silver and other minerals; it's a huge investment."

I called up my broker and told him I wanted to buy the stock. He said, "Okay. Where did you hear about it?" Now, my friend the banker had made it seem like it was a secret—he was telling me off the record, so to speak. I didn't want to get him in trouble, so I didn't go into details, I just said, "A friend told me."

That right there was a warning sign I should have heeded. I should at least have done my own research. But it was the early 1960s, I was still learning, and I bought the stock. I put $300 into it, which was worth a lot more back then, especially on what I was earning. Anyway, I put the money in, and I waited. And waited. I was sure it was going to jump.

The stock didn't budge.

Then there was news of a board meeting. There was finally going to be some movement, so I waited some more . . . and it started to go down. My investment sank from $300 to $250 to $200. When it hit $100, I finally got out. I lost two-thirds of my investment.

It was a good, if expensive, lesson to learn.

Hot tips are a joke. Anytime it seems like someone's letting you in on something under the table, that's a good time to walk away. And of course, always have that other foot on solid ground. I had other investments; that $300 was not my entire portfolio. I didn't sell everything to pour it all into this one hot tip, that's a very important point. It came from my working capital. You can make mistakes, just make them cautiously.

Honestly, a lot of what I'm about to tell you is common sense. I've taken what I've learned from my own mistakes and from the successes and advice of others. You should do the same: Learn from many people, but most of all from your own financial wins and misadventures.

Okay? Great. With the explicit understanding that I am not telling you to follow this advice, but only giving you a glimpse into my own litmus test, here is what I do before I buy stock.

## Find the Company's Price-to-Earnings Ratio (P/E)

Sometimes simple math is the most basic way to understand how any company is doing financially, and the price-to-earnings ratio (P/E) gives you a way to compare any company to its competitors or to the market in general. It is the *price* of a single share of stock divided by the company's *earnings* per share of stock.

Let's actually take a step back.

The price of a single share of stock is obvious. It's what you can buy it for today, right now. And it changes, sometimes minute by minute.

The earnings per share (EPS) is a little trickier. First, you can look at how well the company performed over the last year; this number is based on past earnings, so it is called the *trailing P/E*. This is a critical number and the first thing I look at. It tells you how much investors are willing to invest in the company per dollar of that company's earnings.

This is the part you have to get your head around: It is not a reflection of how well the company is doing financially. It is a reflection of how much investors believe in the company's potential to make money. Sometimes, people call this the "price multiple," because it reflects how many times (or at what multiple) the company's earnings people are willing to pay to invest in it. I'll do the math with some examples in a moment so you can see what I mean, but it's not uncommon for healthy, growing companies to trade their stock at fifteen or twenty times their earnings.

That first ratio, the trailing P/E, uses an earnings number based on past performance. But there is a second ratio I always look at; this one uses the company's projections of how well it will do in the coming year. When you divide the stock price by that hypothetical earnings number, it will give you the *forward P/E*.

Both ratios have their limitations: The trailing P/E has older numbers, so it might not reflect the company's current situation, while the forward P/E is more of an estimate. It is, however, interesting to look at the two as a snapshot of what analysts expect the stock to do. I promised you some math to make this clearer, so let's look at some simple numbers to show you what I mean.

- A company's stock is $100/share.
- Their earnings over the last year were $8/share.
- Price $\div$ earnings = $100 \div 8 = 12.5$

In other words, the company is trading for 12.5 times its trailing earnings. Which doesn't mean much without context, but that is the beauty of P/E. You can do the same math for all the companies in their line of business to see how they compare. You can even compare it to an index like the S&P 500, whose trailing P/E is made up of all the companies it tracks (in the first quarter of 2024, its P/E was roughly 22).

You also need to understand whether it's good or bad to be trading for five times your earnings or twenty-two times your earnings or even fifty times your earnings, and that's where things get a little confusing, but stay with me. The higher the P/E, the more investors believe the company is poised for growth, which makes sense: The stock price is a reflection of how eager investors are to buy it. They obviously would be willing to pay more because they believe it's going to grow.

But sometimes investors "overvalue" a company. Conventional wisdom is that you want a company to be trading somewhere between ten- and twenty-times earnings (and some analysts think the S&P 500's P/E of 22 is as high as you would want to go). A P/E of 12.5 places our imaginary company right where one would expect for it to be poised for growth.

Let's say that suddenly the stock price shot up to $400/share; if that happened, the math would look very different. Now the P/E is 50, well over that twenty-times-earnings benchmark. Is it overvalued or did the company suddenly reveal new and exciting potential? This is also where you could look at past trailing P/E ratios for the company to see when all this enthusiasm kicked in (and whether or not the company has made good on its potential in the past) or compare it to the forward P/E to see if analysts believe earnings will go up (in which case the P/E will go *down* as the denominator [projected earnings] gets bigger).

There is one additional P/E ratio that I always want to look at, and that is the *price/earnings-to-growth (PEG) ratio*. You take the company's trailing P/E ratio and divide that by the anticipated growth rate of its earnings, often over a significant period of time, such as the next five years. This can help you see past a stock's high P/E ratio when it also has a high growth rate. Something that looks overvalued may be, in fact, a good buy.

Let's go back to our earlier example. Our sample company is trading for $400/share, with earnings of $8/share and a trailing P/E of 50. If the projected growth for its earnings over the next five years is 20 percent, then its PEG ratio is 50 divided by 20, or 2.5. For context, you want the PEG ratio to be under 1.0, so 2.5 means the company is probably not going to grow fast enough to make it worth investing at this stock price. It is *overvalued*. If, however, the projected growth of their earnings for the next five years is 55 percent, then the numbers look better: 50 divided by 55 is 0.9, which is below 1.0. At a $400/

share price and a trailing P/E of 50, it may look as though our imaginary company is vastly overvalued, yet the PEG lets us see that it may in fact be a good buy.

This ratio is very useful when comparing companies within the same industry. Their stock prices and trailing P/E ratios can vary widely, but the PEG can bring everything together so that you are comparing one number and a very clear bar: which ones have the smallest PEG, ideally under 1.0?

The only thing to keep in mind is that the earnings growth rate is a projection, an estimation. Different analysts will come up with different numbers and none of them may be exactly right. This is one of the reasons why pundits get so worked up when a company exceeds or misses its projected earnings for a quarter: It throws their predictions out of whack. We forget that nobody really knows what's going to happen until it happens. Useful as it is, even the PEG should only be one tool in your toolbox when it comes to analyzing a potential investment.

If the company has not made money and the earnings per share of stock is zero or less than zero, there will be no P/E listed for the stock. You can't divide by zero, so there is no ratio to report. In this case, a lack of trailing P/E gives you very interesting information indeed. You may believe it's poised to grow, but I would want more than belief before I poured my money into the company's stock. To start with, I would want the company to have a solid plan for how they're going to start becoming profitable before they run out of cash.

I like a P/E ratio that suggests investor confidence that earnings will go up. A high P/E ratio means investors have faith in the company. It doesn't make sense to me to buy something that is wildly overvalued, however, as it can be hard to recoup that investment. I don't want a company to have to slay dragons for the stock price to go up even more. On the other hand, I'm not interested in a very low P/E ratio, which would indicate that stock prices are declining.

Let's say the stock price dipped to $40/share. Now the trailing P/E is $40 divided by $8, which gives us a P/E of 5. Either the stock is a terrific bargain or no one has any faith that its earnings are poised to grow, and they are dumping stock as fast as they can.

You make money when a company grows, but also when you sell your stock for a higher price than you bought it for. For that to happen, other investors must also believe in the company and be willing to pay more than you did for their stock. Check the PEG ratio—do analysts believe the company has the potential for double-digit growth? Also, take a quick reality check: Is the problem market-wide or did just that one stock lose 90 percent of its value? If so, why, and is the problem fatal?

Look, I don't need to be smarter than all the other investors. I don't need to bet on a long shot to prove that I know more. I like to make confident choices in companies whose business models I understand. I don't follow the crowd—there's no money to be made in buying today's latest fad—but I don't need to buck the trends either. It's not a game; I'm not competing with anyone. I take investing seriously because at the end of the day, the only thing that matters is that my money has grown.

> *Here's how I think of my money: soldiers. I send them out to war every day. I want them to take prisoners and come home so there's more of them.*
> —Kevin O'Leary

You can see how P/E ratios can be useful tools, especially when comparing many different companies in the same business space. They can help you see whether there's one company that is perhaps over-priced compared to its competitors or whether there's a lot of potential for growth in the entire industry. But you can also see how, by itself, the P/E ratio doesn't give you enough information. Is the company truly poised for growth or just the latest fad?

We need more data.

## Reading the Prospectus

I mentioned earlier that you can find a company's prospectus online, but you can also get it from your broker or reach out to the company directly and have it mailed or emailed to you. No matter how you get it, the important thing is to read it. Or at least scan it for the key information.

The most direct understanding of a company can be found in its prospectus, as I mentioned. Usually, extensive information is available there about the financial condition of the company. Keep in mind that you're not just looking for profitable companies; you are looking to diversify (there's that word again) within your portfolio by mixing up the level of aggression in the companies you take on.

## Diversifying Stocks by Level of Aggression

Studying a prospectus helps me figure out what to expect from a company. This is broadly generalized, but I find there are three types of motivations that drive the aggression of a company, and you can discern which they are from the material they provide:

- **Aggressive companies.** These usually have high P/E ratios because of the expectation that they will have a great future—and make investors a great deal on expected earnings. Everyone wants to be in on these, which helps the company to have a higher-than-usual growth pattern. Their higher market value comes with a higher risk level. These companies often try to beat out the competition by breaking new ground. They are "disrupters," bringing a new approach and (often) new technology to the fore. They tend to be younger companies, and they also usually limit dividends. Instead, they are plowing that money back into their business.

  Grow-grow-grow is the drumbeat of an aggressive company. It is wonderful to have some of these stocks in your portfolio because they can drive wealth. But be smart! If you don't understand their business model, it could be because they don't really have one. I have a friend who invested in Helios and Matheson Analytics when they bought MoviePass because she couldn't believe they didn't have a plan to monetize the massive number of subscribers signing up. She just assumed she wasn't smart enough to see what they had in mind. Sadly, it quickly became clear that they really didn't have a plan; they burned through their cash faster than they could monetize the millions of new subscribers. The company eventually went bankrupt, and she lost her investment.

- **Conservative companies.** These protect your wealth. Generally older, stable companies with little to no debt, conservative companies are an important way to preserve wealth even during economic downturns. They generally offer limited dividends but also little risk. You want to think of household names, companies that you personally couldn't do without. They are not exciting; they are generally not innovative. What they are is unlikely to crash and burn. You want to have a couple of these in your portfolio so that you are not devastated financially by an economic downturn.

- **Middle-of-the-road companies.** You want to add moderate companies to your portfolio to balance growth and dividends. Moderate companies combine some aggressive behaviors with the firmer footing of conservative companies. There is expected growth on all fronts: increasing sales, profits, and dividends. They seek out new opportunities to do what they are already good at. They are not out to change the world themselves, perhaps, but they are developing right along with it.

A final word about growth rate. It can be tempting to make every decision in your portfolio based on a company's projected growth. Your shares will never increase in market value unless the company is expanding. Growth looks like many things: A company could be innovating in new products, optimizing its core business for increased profits, consolidating to improve its net worth, acquiring or merging with others for a combined greater potential for growth . . . .

Prioritizing growth rate seems like an obvious step.

But with growth comes risk. For one thing, everyone may be hopping on the bandwagon, driving the stock price up in a frenzy when a more moderate approach is advisable. Pay attention to the company's share price and its P/E ratio. Figure out its PEG ratio. If the price of a share of stock rises faster than the company's growth rate, there could be disappointment ahead. What does the profit and loss statement look like? How much money does it have on hand? A company has to have enough cash to see it through the bumpy parts of the road. It has to be able to stay in business long enough to turn that projected growth into real earnings that refill the coffers. How much debt is it carrying? Is repaying that debt going to stifle its ability to make important improvements?

When I say you should invest in companies you understand, I mean you should know a little something about the business they are in. Are good times ahead industry-wide, or is the equivalent of the invention of the motor car on the horizon poised to disrupt the growth of every horse and buggy LLC?

The stock market is not rocket science. It is regular people trying to make things that other people need. Those things can be computers or medicine or donuts. You get to be part of their success by helping finance them through the purchase of shares of stock in their company. Isn't that amazing? America's economy is built on the participation of everyone. We are all in this together.

Your part of the bargain is to use your intelligence to research and your empathy to understand the companies that catch your eye before you buy their stock. Growth is one factor among many. Only you know what's right for your goals. Please don't rely on people whose job is to sound smart on TV to make your financial decisions for you.

This takes us back to the topic of information you can find about a company.

## Reading a Profit and Loss Statement

The prospectus is *not* the best place to find the profit and loss statement. The SEC requires companies to make that statement public every quarter; you want to look at the most recent one, and you'll be able to find that on the same SEC.gov website I mentioned earlier. Search the company and look for the most recent quarterly report. The financial information will be there. Again, you can also ask your broker for the information or (often) find it on the company's website.

At the top of the quarterly report will be the company's revenue. You can see exactly how much money they made. Below that will be many lines of expenses. The numbers themselves may be in thousands or millions, depending on the size of the company. It can be interesting to see where their money goes, but you don't need to parse every line (although if that's your thing, don't let me stop you). At the bottom, it will give you the net income/(loss) for the company as well as per share. If that number is profit, it will appear in plain type: 64,020 or 5,174 (again, except for the per-share amounts, these figures are in thousands or millions of dollars; the statement will tell you which it is at the very top).

If, however, the company *has* lost money, then the figures will appear in parenthesis, such as (14,025) or (10,943). This means the company was not profitable. They are losing money. That will be reflected in the per-share price as well—for instance as (0.03) or (0.08), meaning an earnings per share loss of three cents or eight cents. This is not the same as the stock's share price, which may still go up or down depending on how much investors believe the company can turn the ship around.

If the company is making money, great! That's what you want to see. You can compare how much it made over the same time period last year to see how it's growing; that information is right there in the financial statement, next to this year's numbers. There are several possibilities: Even if the company is making money, company growth could be steady, increasing, or slowing. Obviously, you hope for steady or increasing growth.

> *The essence of math is not to make simple things complicated, but to make complicated things simple.*
> —Stan Gudder

Next, take a look at their balance sheet, which you will find in the same quarterly report. Don't be too concerned about their total assets; what you really want to know is how much cash they have on hand. Again, some historical information will be right there—you will be able to see their numbers from the end of the prior year. If the company is losing money, this is invaluable information: You can see how quickly they are burning through their cash and how much of it they have left. This, in turn, will let you know how long they may be able to hold out before going bankrupt.

Does that sound harsh? Math is remorseless. There is nowhere to hide in these financial disclosures. To use simple numbers, if a company is losing $1 million a year, and they have $100 million in cash, then they have a hundred years to figure out a solution. Plenty of time. But if they only have $2 million in cash, they may not have enough time or wiggle room to find a solution or adjust to new realities. It takes money to pivot something as large as a multimillion-dollar business; if a company is low on cash, they are losing agility as well as running out of time.

Debt structure along with cash structure should be compared as well. You want to make sure the value of the company is protected. Are the debts covered realistically? If the debts are to help the business grow, will the projected additional income be enough to pay them off? If so, debt is not a problem. Just as with your own personal finance, taking on debt to be able to expand your business or buy a house or a rental property—something that will increase in value—is good debt. Putting a vacation on a credit card at over 20 percent interest rate is bad debt, in that what you bought won't appreciate, the terms of your debt are high, and you may or may not have a plan for how you will pay it back. Be cautious around companies who do the equivalent.

Whether a company is making or losing money, how it's been performing over time, its rate of growth, and its cash on hand are all critical pieces of information you can glean in fifteen minutes of reading the most recent quarterly report. It is well worth your time. If you want to get into more detail, there is much more information to be found there. You can go deep into exactly how the company spends its money, what the profit margins are on its key products, and what the executives have to say about their plans for the future.

Again, if you invest in industries where you already understand the basics, you have an edge. You can see where there is potential and where, perhaps, a company is poised to fail. Play to your strengths, at least at the beginning. At the very least, be willing to learn.

Never rationalize a bad investment. Don't waste time justifying why you bought a stock. You don't have to make yourself into a villain for choosing a stock that is not living up to your expectations. Move on! Sell the stock, take your loss, learn from the experience. Make new decisions going forward. Rationalizing is a waste of time and energy, and denial will keep you stuck with a bad decision. You have to stay open, be willing to reevaluate where you are, and move into new opportunities. Markets fluctuate; a smart investor uses every experience, positive and negative, to come up with new approaches and make better decisions down the line.

## Other Considerations in My Litmus Test

I have already talked about dividends at length. I like companies that pay dividends, but more than that, I like whatever dividend policy the board of directors may have to be something that increases the share value of your stock. That's the most important thing—that the decisions are made with an eye toward increasing the value of the company and the stock over the long term. Which brings me to my final consideration: the people involved.

Before investing in a company, I take a good, long look at who their chief executive officer (CEO) is. First, I look for what might be wrong with them:

- Did they come up the ranks in another industry? Basing decisions on past experience from a different industry can be a disaster.

- Are they failing to keep up with the changes? These can be broad changes in society and the global marketplace, or smaller (but no less important) niche-specific changes.

- Are they creating excessive debt?

- What is their ability to negotiate with unions?

To me, successful CEOs:

- Promote morale among their employees.

- Develop new products.

- Consider the impact their decisions have on both the short term and the long term (for instance, not saddling their future business with stifling debt).

- Maintain a positive image for themselves and their company in the market.

The best thing, I think, about my litmus test is that it's easy to understand. I know some computer-savvy investors these days run complicated algorithms to choose a stock. If that works for you, don't let me stop you! But my litmus test is all about the fundamentals. Who are the people making the big decisions and do they know what they're doing? Is the company making money? Do they have enough in reserve to handle a sudden reversal of fortune? Are they poised for growth?

> *Investing isn't about beating others at their game.*
> *It's about controlling yourself at your own game.*
> —Benjamin Graham

I know a lot of lucky investors who used their intuition and succeeded. I'm happy for them, but the problem with this approach is that they believe they are invincible, that their gut will always make a great decision. What they are is lucky, but believing your luck is some kind of innate skill prevents you from putting together a real investment strategy; it makes it easy to avoid doing the real work. But if all you are doing in the stock market is gambling, sooner or later the house always wins—and you lose.

Longtime successful investors use meticulous strategies, analyzing and revisiting their decisions. Their willingness to admit mistakes and make better choices helps them stay flexible for the long term. They put in the work to stay aware of changing trends in the market and they show discipline, not jumping from one stock to another based on the latest craze being promoted.

And don't kid yourself—there are a lot of crazy crazes out there. Whenever there is money involved, an abundance of crystal-ball promoters will come out of the woodwork. It was once said, "Figures don't lie; liars figure." They will have very plausible-sounding reasons to follow their advice—especially if you have to pay for it.

Having said that, I have a lot of friends who are investors who have what I would call unusual reasons for investing in one company over another. I don't think anyone is going to argue with "Buy low, sell high." Behind that simple phrase, however, is a lot of work.

To successfully "buy low," you have to analyze a lot of stocks to see which ones might be undervalued. I have friends who focus on depressed stocks, researching their fundamentals, why they might be depressed, and which ones are poised to get back to their former prices. Sometimes there are resource shortages, litigation, government regulations, or a million other things that time alone might eventually correct. These friends keep cash on hand, waiting for an opening that suggests the negative situation is on the mend. Knowing the reason behind the low value allows you to anticipate future possibility. It's not luck—it's hard work.

Similarly, "sell high" sounds easy, but it's difficult to sell a stock that everyone else wants to buy. If your emotions are involved, you're likely to hang onto the stock until it starts to go down again—and maybe even then. I have friends who constantly evaluate their positions, looking for stocks they believe are overvalued. Some decide ahead of time what that price might be, and when the stock hits it, they sell.

And then there are more interesting strategies. It's great fun to talk to investors and get their take on the best way to invest. There are so many different approaches. I had a friend who would predict which car manufacturer would do best by testing the new models that came out each year. When he found a particular model that he thought would do great, he would go all in, pouring 100 percent of his investment into that manufacturer. He may have been crazy (he definitely didn't diversify, so don't follow his example!), but I'll tell you what—he was successful.

Another friend would base his investments on the most successful executives. Again, he wasn't crazy; he too was successful. The leadership of a company is a major force in the success of a company. My friend was great with people—he understood them the way my other friend understood cars. Perhaps a key takeaway is to lean into your own strengths.

A good friend who worked with me as a consultant specialized in corporations that were debt sensitive. When interest rates were low, he would buy their stock; lower interest rates gave these companies more room to maneuver and a better chance at survival. He expected that when the interest rates were climbing, a debt-sensitive company would feel the heat first and the company's profit would decrease, so he would sell the stock before that happened.

These were all people with a great deal of experience in the stock market. I don't recommend going all in on any one strategy when you're starting out (or ever, unless that one strategy is diversification, which is always a good idea).

Value investing is all about getting to the intrinsic value of a common stock, independent of its market price. It helps you make decisions outside of the noise around this or that hot topic. Following the crowd that brought the market price up or down can be a dangerous strategy; you'll always be behind. The crowd itself could be making false assumptions and miscalculations. Taking small steps and easing into an investment may not produce the greatest gain, but it will prevent one from taking a big loss.

You are responsible for your choices. Don't be led by vague information, especially when there's excellent real information at your fingertips.

Picking up this book was a great step in educating yourself. I urge you to keep going. There are smart people out there with a lot to teach you, and sometimes just hearing them disagree can be an education! I learned a lot from the "father of value investing," Benjamin Graham, who wrote two foundational books: *Security Analysis* (co-written with David Dodd, 1934) and *The Intelligent Investor* (1949). He developed criteria for stock analysis that holds up to this day (in fact, Warren Buffett was one of his students). Once again, learn from many, but follow none blindly.

# What Is an IPO?

An IPO, or initial public offering, is when a stock is available for purchase for the first time.

Many companies are privately held, which means you and I can't buy stock in them. But some companies reach a point where they are ready and willing to trade on the exchange. That first offering of stock is the IPO.

In the last year, there have been over a hundred new IPOs. Returns on those stocks, if you'd bought them on day 1, would range from +364 percent to −100 percent. You read that right: For some companies, the stock is now worthless. Not just within a year, but for some, within a month of their IPO.

IPOs tend to be hyped by brokerage companies that have a vested interest in selling the stock for their own profit.

As with any unproven stock, IPOs come with potential high rewards but equally high risks. Evaluate them carefully.

ROBERT BARBERA

# Diversifying Stocks by Sector

The stock market is divided into sectors, which are basically different types of industries. You want to have your investments in more than one industry so you're not exposed if some massive industry upset occurs. A recession or depression will lower the whole stock market, but often one particular industry will be hit harder than most. Think of when the Dotcom Bubble burst in 2000, or when the housing bubble, fueled by subprime mortgages, burst in 2008. Everything in the market might take a hit as the dust settles, but the industry at the center of the crisis takes the biggest hit.

Diversifying by sector backstops your investments in a crisis. Consumer Staples may hold up while Real Estate tumbles, or Energy may take a hit but Communication Services remains sound. Change is inevitable.

There are eleven stock market sectors, according to the Global Industry Classification Standard (GICS). They are:

- Energy
- Materials
- Industrials
- Utilities
- Healthcare
- Financials
- Consumer Discretionary
- Consumer Staples
- Information Technology
- Communication Services
- Real Estate

You might think these divisions are set in stone, but in fact they're fluid. Real Estate, for instance, used to be considered part of the Financials sector. Communication Services is a relatively new way of looking at the connections between telecommunications companies and media/entertainment in the age of streaming.

Diversifying stocks by sector isn't about being in every sector or the "right" sector. It's about owning stock in companies that line up with your financial goals *and* are in a few different sectors. Everything in your portfolio is aligned with your vision, and you are wise enough to diversify your stocks so that a run on tech stocks won't wipe you out.

A quick aside here: Only you can decide when to sell your stock, but I would be remiss if I didn't remind you that panic is a terrible emotion to act on. If the ship truly is sinking, then by all means jump into a lifeboat. But many stocks have gone down only to go back up again. In 2008, the Dow Jones Industrial Average lost a third of its value, falling from 13,264 at the end of 2007 to only 8,776 points at the end of 2008. By the end of 2023, it had bounced back and galloped past its previous high to a whopping 37,689 points. Not every company survived that crisis, but those that did came back strong.

Revisit a company's fundamentals before making any decision to sell low. You still get to do it if you decide that selling is the best solution! But you should know why each stock is in your portfolio in the first place and revisit on a regular basis whether you believe it is still a good investment. That way, when (not if) a crisis occurs—or when (not if) the market as a whole becomes overheated and poised to go down—you can make an informed decision about when and at what price you want to sell.

> *If you must play, decide on three things*
> *at the start: the rules of the game, the*
> *stakes, and the quitting time.*
>
> —Chinese proverb

## Diversifying Stocks by Size

Stocks are divided into categories by size. The size of a company has an impact on its potential for growth and on its stability.

My own portfolio investment strategy (which is not by any means the only investment strategy—follow your own North Star), breaks down like this:

- **Large-Capitalization Stocks—40%**
  *Capitalization and growth*

As the name implies, large-cap stocks are shares of companies that are well-established. They are well-known and have a huge market capitalization of more than $10 billion. (Market capitalization is determined by multiplying all outstanding shares of stock by the stock price.) These companies generally have less risk because they are, well, behemoths. Examples of these companies would include General Motors, AT&T, and FedEx—all household names (I'm not endorsing these, by the way, but merely showing you examples). They are easy to find: The S&P 500 tracks only the 500 largest companies as defined by their market capitalization.

The downside to these companies is that they have already grown so much; aggressive growth tends to be in smaller companies. But the upside is that they are proven winners. Just remember you never want all your money in just one part of the market. For one thing, you might miss out on nimble newcomers with high growth potential. For another, technology continues to develop at a dizzying pace, which opens the possibility for disruption. Xerox used to be an iconic company, a legitimate worldwide powerhouse. It had been around for 115 years and had looked untouchable for a good chunk of its lifespan . . . until it limped to its end in 2018. What brought down a company so synonymous with copying documents that its name had become a verb? It was too big and slow and lumbering to adapt to rapidly changing technology. Large companies can bring stability, but they can also be dangerously set in their ways. They are a part of your portfolio, but should not be the only thing you invest in.

- **Mid-Capitalization Stocks—40%**
  *Lower-expectation value investments*

  The companies in this range are more likely than the bigger, more established companies to be growth-oriented. Their market capitalization falls in the range of $2 billion to $10 billion. They are still developing, which, yes, can be riskier, but also potentially more profitable. At the same time, they are not brand-new or untested. They straddle the line between risky startups and plodding dinosaurs—although you need to do your research. Some mid-caps are on their way down from having been large-cap stocks, not on their way up to greatness. They also tend to do more business domestically, whereas large-cap companies tend to be more global in nature. Some examples of mid-cap stocks (again, not recommendations, just examples) would be The Gap, Walgreens, and Wyndham Hotels & Resorts. Several indexes follow just mid-cap stocks, including the S&P MidCap 400 Index.

- **Small-Capitalization Stocks—20%**
  *Riskier, growth-oriented, may provide adequate diversification*

  Diversification means including a few stocks that have the potential for exceptional growth. Smaller ($300 million to $2 billion in market capitalization), often newer, less-tried-and-true companies can present opportunities, but with those opportunities come risk. Be warned: Their share prices tend to be very volatile and sometimes they disappoint. Amazon started out as a small-cap stock, but so did Chicken Soup for the Soul Entertainment; Nevada Copper, Inc; and Fisker, Inc.—all of which filed for bankruptcy this year. You must always look to your own capacity to tolerate risk before you make any investment decision.

This seems like a good moment to remind you of defining your own goals as you put together your stock portfolio. I've gone on a lot about risk because it is inherent in every aspect of life, and perhaps none more so than in your financial investments. It's important to look at your goals, but at the same time, you can't make a plan without being honest about your risk tolerance.

My personal goal has always been to get a 10 percent return on my investments. Historically, that's right around what the S&P 500 has averaged over the course of its existence. That means I need to be as diverse in my investments as the S&P 500 or the stock market itself. I have to be willing to take some risks. In fact, I have a very high capacity to embrace risk—as my late wife, Bernice, would attest to, since more than once I left a job without having another lined up, or spent down to our last $25 to purchase an apartment complex that was a stretch, to say the least.

If you have no tolerance for risk, I hope to convince you that putting your money in Treasury bonds or a savings account at your local bank is NOT the same as taking no risks. As I mentioned earlier, you will predictably lose purchasing power—which amounts to losing money—if your interest rate is below the inflation rate. For people who expect to be on fixed incomes in retirement, this is a disastrous strategy.

On the other hand, something like investing in a new startup might mean getting in on the ground floor of a multibillion-dollar, industry-disrupting business. The potential return on investment in these situations might be enormous—if, that is, the business is a "unicorn" like Airbnb or Uber. Or the startup could very well go belly-up and investors might lose everything. The potential risk is extremely high. Most startups do fail within a few years. According to the website Failory.com, 75 percent of venture-backed companies never return cash to investors, and in half of those cases, investors end up losing their entire investment. Obviously, you do not want to take a risk like this with money you know you're going to need. Don't bet the rent money.

Venture capitalists with enormous amounts of money to invest still diversify, spreading their investments across many promising startups. They're doing the same kind of thing I hope you'll do in the stock market: putting their money behind different types of companies so the winners balance out the losers, and readjusting when they have better data.

The stock market does not have to be only feast or famine! There can be a middle ground. I know experts who want you to aim for a 4 percent or 5 percent annual return on investment, which is very doable. Again, the S&P 500 has averaged a 10.26 percent return since its inception in 1957. As long as your returns remain above inflation—which, as I write these words in mid-2024, stands at 2.9 percent—you will make money. Your nest egg will grow. You will come out ahead, which is the key goal.

*All money means to me is a pride in accomplishment.*
—Ray Kroc

For me, earning 10 percent annually makes me happy. That's the only word for it. I rest easy knowing my money is working hard for me and that my family is provided for. But maintaining that return does involve a certain active participation; you have to be willing to do the research, understand the stocks, cut your losses and put your time, money, and attention on better-performing companies. To me, this is fun! I love the challenge. I love watching my investments go up and down (although I love up more than down!). The research, staying on top of things—it all gets my blood flowing. At the same time, I understand it's not everyone's idea of a good time. It can be a lot of work.

There is a shortcut, and that is mutual funds.

## Mutual Funds

If you don't have the time or interest in staying on top of the market, one way to avoid having to do research on individual stocks—as well as diversify your holdings and simply save time—is to invest in a mutual fund.

The fund managers take care of all the records, analyze risks, and generally make your decisions for you—for a fee. There is a wide selection of funds to meet every possible sector and risk profile. There are different fee structures, including a potential upfront commission, which is referred to as a "load." There are both load and no-load funds. All funds also charge a fee that is a percentage of your investment; the word you're looking for is "expense ratio," and it varies widely. Both fees may come out of the money you invest. Loads are especially disliked by some investors for eating away at their initial investment—taking their money off the top, as it were.

I go into a little more depth in the next sidebar, but as a very general statement, you want to look for the no-load mutual funds that have the lowest expense ratios. This is how you keep most of your money working for you. But again, you make the choice. What you are trading off is that the lower the expense ratio, the more likely the fund is to be an index or a passively managed fund. The higher expense ratio goes to paying experts to actively manage the fund—which doesn't mean they are infallible. The fund may offer higher potential returns, but they remain more expensive on an ongoing basis. And remember, those higher returns are "potential." Nothing is guaranteed. In fact, I have a cautionary tale coming up!

Only you can decide what makes sense for your portfolio. It doesn't need to be either/or; you can invest in different funds for different personal objectives.

All mutual funds supply investors with their history, which of course is no guarantee of future returns. I would take this an extra step and compare it to how well the S&P 500 did over the same time period, just to have a point of reference.

There are many positives of mutual funds. Some pass along dividends from the stocks they hold to fund investors. Others are designed to minimize dividends for tax reasons. You get to pick a fund that works best for you. Even more important, you can be a small investor and easily invest in several funds, creating a diverse portfolio with relatively little initial investment. There are funds to meet every objective and objection; some funds go all in on one particular industry, while others studiously avoid certain types of companies.

In an actively managed fund, all the companies they buy shares in are analyzed by experts to meet the fund's goals. In an index fund, they follow an index (like the S&P 500 or the Dow Jones Industrial

Average) so you do as well as that segment of the market does. Actively managed funds are generally more expensive than passively managed index funds. That expense can come in the form of loads (commissions) and expense ratios, which take a cut of the entire value of your fund investment. Obviously, lower fees equal more of your money actively working for you. Some (but not all) actively managed funds do better than passively managed, low-fee index funds (more on those below.) Do your own research to see what makes sense for you.

Every fund will give you statistics on its historical performance, from which you can glean how aggressive/risky it may be and the potential upside it has for propulsive growth. There may be room in your portfolio for mutual funds with different philosophies, fee structures, and goals.

In addition, mutual funds are huge; they represent an enormous investment in the market and can have a significant impact on the shares they invest in. They buy in a big way if the market is doing well and sell in a big way when the market is not doing well. The mutuals report to investors on a regular basis, and they are very liquid: If your goals change or you feel you want to own fewer (or more) shares of the fund, you can rapidly liquidate or increase your stake.

Having given you the good news, let me also give you the bad. You will hear a lot about mutual funds that do well, beating the market and generally taking Wall Street by storm. You will hear a lot less about the ones that don't do well, returning far less than the market average. Some funds do better than others, so it's always worth researching funds before you invest. You can be less involved in stock picking when you have a mutual fund, but you still need to be willing to do the work to make an informed decision.

I myself was taken in by the hype around a certain fund manager. When he was opening up a new mutual fund, major financial news outlets talked up his financial wizardry. How could I go wrong?

You know how this story ends.

To say that his new fund, into which I had invested quite a bit of money, was lackluster would be an understatement. When the fund did not do well, I did a little more digging. What I discovered was that this fellow made a habit of starting new funds with different investment criteria—one of which did spectacularly well and was reported on, as I'd seen, glowingly in the press. But the vast majority of them did not do well; of those, I heard nary a peep in the financial news. He wasn't a financial wizard—he was just a so-so stock picker who won big once. That's a gambler, not an investor, and definitely not someone I want picking stocks on my behalf. I got out of the fund.

You can lose money in a mutual fund just as you can lose money in individual stocks. This is always true; the market WILL go down. The trick is to not need the money until it has a chance to go back up. Which, so far, it always has, although words to live by are "past history is not a guarantee of future success."

The key is to not be forced into selling at a loss—one of the many ways in which having time is your friend in the stock market. I'll talk more about your investment horizon when I talk about portfolios. But if you are assuming that the market will only ever go up, you are simply wrong. Mutual funds may help you to diversify, but there is no foolproof path to ever-increasing wealth. We try to minimize our lumps, but we'll still have to take 'em.

> *Honesty is the fastest way to prevent a*
> *mistake from turning into a failure.*
> —James Altucher

## Open-End Mutual Funds

Most mutual funds are open-end funds. That means an unlimited number of shares are available for purchase. You buy directly from the investment firm behind the fund and sell back to them as well. The price is based on the fund's net asset value (NAV), which is simply their assets minus any liabilities; you get the net asset value per share (NAVPS) by dividing the NAV by the number of outstanding shares. Pretty simple math.

Open-end mutual funds tend to be relatively stable, but also have lower potential returns than closed-end funds. There are some other downsides as well. Although the fund's per-share price may fluctuate during the day, all trades are executed at the NAV price, which is only calculated at the end of the trading day. So the price you see on the fund in the morning, when you decide to sell, may not be the exact price you get when the trade is executed at the end-of-day NAVPS.

Also, because of how easy they are to redeem—and remember, there are unlimited shares of them—they need to keep a chunk of their assets in a cash reserve to cover redemptions. This means they can't invest a percentage of their assets (i.e., a percentage of your investment) in something that will appreciate; they have to keep it in cash.

They are not without risk. A run on the fund, in which there are suddenly a lot of redemptions, can drain their cash reserves and force them to sell stock assets, sometimes at a loss, driving down the NAV. But they are generally considered less risky than closed-end funds, which we will look at now.

## Closed-End Mutual Funds

Closed-end mutual funds offer a fixed number of shares at an initial public offering. Unlike open-end funds, they are closed—hence the name—to new investment and capital. You don't redeem them by selling them back to the investment firm, the way you do with shares of open-end funds, which means they don't need to keep vast cash reserves. They can invest all of their assets in stocks, and they often focus on areas where there is higher potential return. And what do we know about higher returns? The trade-off is nearly always a higher risk, and that is true here as well.

If you don't sell shares back to the investment firm, how do you sell them? The answer is that you sell on the exchange, as if it were a stock. This means you can get exactly the price you see at the time you execute the trade (unlike open-end funds, which are only priced and traded at the end of the day). But that also means the price can go up or down, just like a stock.

The value of each share of a closed-end fund varies because of supply (which is limited; unlike open-end funds, there are no new shares) and demand (which can be fickle). If the share price is above the fund's NAVPS, the fund is said to be trading at a premium. If the share price is below the NAVPS, it's said to be trading at a discount.

If you can buy the shares at a discount and sell them at a premium, good for you! It's just like with a stock—you want to buy low and sell high. But as you learned from my own mutual fund misadventure, it is not without risk.

## Load vs. No-Load Mutual Funds

All mutual funds charge fees—which makes sense, since they incur expenses and are providing a service. However, the amount and types of fees vary widely. One difference is that some mutual funds charge a "load," or a commission, usually when you buy the fund shares.

No-load mutual funds do not charge that commission, although you should check to see how long you must hold the shares before selling them to avoid a penalty. There might be fine print, so look for it.

All mutual funds also have an expense ratio, which is an annual fee. It's a percentage of your investment and can range from extremely little in an index fund to a couple of percentage points in an actively managed fund.

You can compare funds and fees at the nonprofit Financial Industry Regulatory Authority: http://tools.finra.org/fund_analyzer

## Index Funds

An index fund is passively managed. That means no one is sitting at a desk, poring over profit and loss statements, deciding when and what to buy and sell. Instead, they simply mimic the stock market or a portion of it, sometimes based on a broad index like the Dow Jones or the Russell 2000, sometimes based on an industry-specific, or sector, index, such as the S&P 500 Health Care index or the Dow Jones Transportation Average, or even something as niche as the U.S. Distillers and Vintners Index. Some are based on the size of the company, like a mid-cap index, rather than one particular sector. As you can see, there are many different kinds of indexes to choose from.

The advantage of this approach is twofold. First, no one is trying to beat the market. This takes away both a level of aggression and a level of risk.

> *There are only two types of investors—those who know they can't make money from market timing, and those who don't know they can't.*
> —Terry Smith

The market has a long history of averaging around 10 percent growth a year. If you can match that, you can do well. Index funds are considered very stable for a long-term investment. Again, the market could go down tomorrow, but as long as you don't need access to that money, you can stick out the bad times to watch it (hopefully) bounce back to recoup and more. That long horizon evens out risk, especially when you are diversified across an entire index, as these funds are. (Reminder: There is no such thing as no risk, and I am not a financial advisor. I'm just helping to educate you on what's available out there. You make your own choices.)

The second benefit of index funds is that they have very low fees. Because they are not actively managed, they don't have the same staff expenses. No-load, low-expense-ratio mutual funds are boring . . . and almost every single financial guru will suggest that you invest at least a percentage of your portfolio in them. Why?

I mentioned it was boring, right?

That is a feature, not a bug. One of the worst things you can do is buy and sell and buy and sell some more. When you attempt to guess what the market will do, what stocks will go up or down, you might just as well gaze into your crystal ball. People will pretend to know, but no one knows for sure.

There's a great line in the movie *The Big Short* where Dr. Michael Burry says of his bet that the bottom would fall out of the housing market: "I may have been early, but I'm not wrong." His angry client replies, "It's the same thing." Ultimately, Burry was right to have shorted the housing market, but it was touch and go. That's always going to be true because the market isn't just numbers—it also reflects actions taken by millions of human beings, and human beings are flawed, emotional, and hard to predict. There may be a drift you can follow, but when it comes to exact predictions, forget it. A mutual fund takes away the incentive to play the market-timing game.

An index fund goes up with the market, which of course means it also goes down with the market. But as we've discussed, over a long period of time, the market has historically gone up by a consistent average that is well above inflation. An index fund can be thought of as a conservative way to get consistent, moderate returns. For me, that 10 percent annual return has always been enough. Even if you want to be more aggressive with part of your portfolio, you still want to have some returns you can rely upon. I'll talk more about different portfolio objectives in a later chapter.

## Exchange-Traded Funds

An exchange-traded fund (ETF) combines the diversification of mutual funds with the ability to trade on the exchange like a stock. ETFs typically have lower operating costs, which are passed on to the investor, are flexible to trade, and provide transparency. Some may be tax efficient, but be wary: ETFs can be built on a basket of stocks and bonds, but also on commodities, emerging markets, etc., all of which have different tax implications. Do your research.

I've bought ETFs several times as a way to broadly get into a sector that I believed would do well. Once, I was sure it was time for utility companies to withstand the pressure of a nervous market due to signs of depression; rather than buy stocks in one or two utilities, I bought an ETF to cover the entire sector. Another time I could see that oil stocks were doing well, so I bought an ETF specializing in oil drilling and distributing. Just like with an individual stock, you want to have a long-term plan and at the same time be willing to get out when you have made enough profit. Stay vigilant on your ETFs just as you would your stocks.

ETFs also offer you a prospectus filled with information to consider:

- Investment objective
- Fund fees and expenses
- Portfolio turnover
- Principal investment strategy
- Principal risk
- Average annual tax return
- Management of the fund
- Portfolio managers
- Purchases and sales of shares
- Tax information
- Payments to broker-dealer and other financial intermediaries

There is virtually no area of concealment in a prospectus. Get comfortable and start reading them. Why? Because doing your homework will save you money.

Even when I was a little kid at Coney Island amusement park, I could see there were people willing to do the research and people willing to lose their money. You see, there was a mechanical game to pick the horse that would win the race. If you bothered to watch a few races before plunking your money down—in other words, do a little research before getting in the game—it was simple to pick the winning horse.

Because the same horse would win all the time.

Most people never noticed, even though the information was out there for all to see. They would pick their horse according to the jockey's colors or whether the horse looked cute. They never focused on what actually mattered.

I'm sorry to say that many people choose stocks the same way. Learn from Coney Island; a little research can save you a lot of money.

ROBERT BARBERA

## Annuities

An annuity is an insurance contract. You either give them a lump sum or you pay premiums, and then at some point, they start paying you out a regular amount of money that you can count on. Sometimes it's for a fixed period; other times it's for the rest of your life—which makes it very attractive as a retirement option to have a regular stream of income.

The other thing about annuities is that they are very flexible; you can tailor them to your particular needs. In fact, there are so many ways to tailor them, you should talk to a financial advisor about all your possible choices if you're even considering buying an annuity. The key thing to understand is that *you* are funding this annuity, so you want to make sure that it's really the best use of your money.

When I was eleven years old, my dad bought an annuity for my brother and one for me. Money was very tight, but Dad wanted his sons to have $1,000 when we were twenty-one years old—a handsome sum at the time. He had a garment factory during those rough years and wanted my brother and me to have a head start financially. When I cashed in the annuity at twenty-one, I was able to reinvest the money, which worked out very well.

And yet, as good as the gift was, I don't believe in annuities these days. The premium invested is not justified for the payoff down the road. There are plenty of people who will disagree with me, so listen to them as well and see what makes the most sense to you. You should also check to see if the people who recommend annuities get a commission for selling you an annuity.

Hey, I'm not saying don't trust. I'm saying trust but verify.

## Stock Options and Margin Investing

I'm going to be upfront with you: Stock options and margin investing are vastly more complicated than anything I have tackled so far in this book. Entire books and college courses have been devoted to teaching how these things work. Before you dive in, know that this kind of high-level trading demands a real education, but I would be remiss not to tell you that it exists. I firmly believe these things should be left to professionals. I'm going to give you a very quick overview, but proceed at your own risk.

In fact, I'm going to start with a couple of personal stories that will show you just how risky it can be.

Like the time I started investing on margin.

Margin investment is a strategy by which you can leverage stock that you don't own yet. It's a form of credit, which means you'll be paying interest. It can be very risky. The stock is held by the broker for the investor at a market price with the expectation that when the price increases, you can take ownership and sell for a profit, paying for the stock at the original price. But if the market value drops, you, the investor, must cover the loss.

If you've read any of my other books, you know how much I love to leverage other people's money. When I was young, I thought it was great to buy stock on margin by just putting a small percentage down to control the stock. What a great leverage tool. If the stock price increased, a larger profit was made on a smaller investment down. I didn't think too much about what would happen if the stock dropped: The investor has to either cover the margin account or be sold out with the loss. That's what happened to me. The margin call came in, the broker sold the shares, and I was wiped out covering the loss. Margins can be risky and expensive; don't play around until and unless you completely understand the ramifications and costs, and you can afford to lose a lot of money.

I've also bought and sold options. An option is a way to pay to have the right to buy or sell shares by a specific date if it reaches a certain price. It can get very complicated, and there are option strategies with marvelous names like "Protective Collar" and "Long Call Butterfly Spread." They sound like characters in a Damon Runyon story, and I'm not going to tell you that it can't be as risky as Harry the Horse rolling the dice.

The upside of buying or selling an option on stock is that it can provide some protection against market pricing. For a small investment, you can essentially tie up shares of a stock at a specific price; if it goes higher than that agreed-upon "strike" price, you still buy at that lower price and then can resell them immediately for a profit. Whereas, if the price goes down, you have only lost that small investment, rather than having shelled out the entire cost of those shares of stock, only to see them lose value. Meanwhile, if you're the one holding the stock, it can protect you because you either sell at your targeted strike price (which should be high enough that you made a profit on your shares) or you retain ownership of shares that didn't grow as much as you expected, but you have the money from the option payment as consolation.

I first heard about option buying by farmers who wanted to protect the price of their crop. It was like insurance for them: they knew they would make a fair price when their crop came to market, assuming the prices stayed high. But if the prices dipped, they had the money from the option to help make up for the fact they were selling low.

At its basic form, it can be a win-win. But there are a lot of moving parts; you absolutely must educate yourself, including talking to people who know what they're doing (and do not have a financial stake in your decision).

Options trading is complicated, and I know when I need help, so I made an agreement with an option specialist to work together. I have a friend in finance who says the best thing that can happen to someone trading in options is that they lose their shirt on their first trade and never do it again. That's not what happened to me. In the first month, we made big. I was excited! After that first month, though, we had continual losses for the next several months, wiping out not only our gains, but losing our initial investment as well.

Never say I haven't been honest with you. You're allowed to go off and make your own mistakes, but I urge you to be very careful around margins and options. Other things to leave to the experts:

- Hedge Funds. They are generally considered risky, and they usually require a hefty investment. I'm not saying people don't profit from hedge funds, only that you should very carefully weigh risk-to-rewards. Earlier this year, a $2 billion hedge fund went bankrupt, and it wasn't the first. Do your due diligence.

- Cryptocurrency. As a digital currency, crypto is very volatile with huge swings in valuation. Some investors have made huge profits, usually by getting out before the currency collapses entirely. The crypto bubble is made up of several different currencies and has burst more than once. In some cases, massive fraud has been alleged. For all I know, it may be the currency of the future, but the jury is still out. What's not in question is that crypto as a field remains extremely volatile. Proceed at your own risk.

- Fads. Look, I love that human beings have imagination! New products and services are always coming along. And there is something very seductive about getting in on the ground floor of an untried stock. It's also where fools jump in. My belief is that if something is going to do well, it will continue to do well. You can jump in later and make a solid gain. You don't have to take a big risk to make a killing in the stock market.

- Leveraged Buyouts (LBO). This is when a company acquires another company using almost entirely borrowed money. They leverage debt, including bonds that are usually junk grade and the acquired company's own assets. As with everything, there's a potential for a significant upside, but only if they manage to navigate the challenges around the buyout.

- Arbitrage. This is what they call it when you buy a product/share in one market and at the same time immediately sell the same product/share in another market, usually at a tiny profit. It's a game of volume, mostly with liquid assets, and it works because there are small differences in different markets.

- Trading in Foreign Exchange Rates (FOREX). Currency is a big asset class, and it is truly a global phenomenon, allowing you to trade twenty-four hours a day during the week. But it's much less regulated than other exchanges. I think it's difficult to predict how other countries' currencies will appreciate, and because the potential exists to buy with leverage, your potential losses could be astronomical. It's kind of the Wild West; don't venture there with money you can't afford to lose in a hurry.

## So Where Does All of This Leave You?

Look, I want you to see how many opportunities there are, all the different ways your money can make money in and around the stock market. But just because I talk about the different kinds of investments doesn't mean I endorse them. I've flat-out said that I don't like annuities, won't buy gold, and don't care much for bonds. But that's me; what's wrong for me may not be wrong for you. Take my advice as you would a friend's. Allow it to make you think twice, but do your own research, consult your own professional advisors, and make your own decisions.

One thing I will say is this: Be careful of shiny objects. Many of the investments I've talked about are incredibly risky. If you don't understand it well enough to be able to put it into your own words and pinpoint everything that can go wrong, leave it to the professionals. Even they can (and do) get things wrong. Remember that fund manager.

The other thing to be aware of is our very human instinct to try to "make up" any loss, often by doing something even riskier with the remaining funds. I read an article by a woman who, with her husband, lost a big chunk of money to a fraudulent financial advisor. Feeling panicky about the need to rebuild their nest egg in a hurry, they put their remaining funds with a different financial guru who promised sky-high returns.

His name? Bernie Madoff.

But you don't have to be the victim of fraud to fall into this trap. A down market or a stock that tanks can cause very real feelings of panic. Of course you want to do something spectacular, score a big coup, to get back to your previous investment balance. And so you contemplate a high-risk strategy.

Just . . . take a breath first.

Remember that one of the great things about America is that we have always bounced back. In investing, time is your biggest friend, and—while past performance is no guarantee of future earnings—it's worth noting that even after the massive cratering of stock prices that took place during the Great Depression, the stock market eventually recovered. Of course, you know your own time horizon best. You get to make up your own mind about what to do. I am not here to tell you how to invest your money. But I will suggest that panic buying, like panic selling, is not the best way to make a decision.

It takes too much risk to cover a loss by trying to make up for the loss on one swoop. For instance, if you have an investment of $1,000, and you were to put it in something fairly low risk, like a mutual fund based on the S&P 500 (in other words, an index fund), over a regular year in the market, you would expect around 10 percent positive earnings on that money. But let's say it was a bad year on the market, and you lost 10 percent instead. Now you don't just want to make back that 10 percent—you want to make back the 10 percent you feel you "should" have earned.

Example:
- $1,000 at 10% normal positive earnings = $1,100
- $1,000 at 10% loss = $900
- Amount needed to recover from where you "should" be = $200

Some of the "smartest" advice you'll hear from the "smartest" people is to take an even greater risk on that money, to "double down" in an attempt to "win" back the $200. That's gambling, pure and simple! It's the same insanity as doubling your bet at the roulette wheel after a loss when you have exactly the same chance of losing that money as you did before. The roulette wheel doesn't care if you've won or lost! The odds don't change. Nothing shifts in your favor when you place a new bet, and nothing shifts in your favor by putting more money on the same risky strategy.

People will say things to you like "It has to go up sometime" or "You can't lose every hand." But in fact, the stock or fund or what have you does NOT have to go up. Hundreds of companies go bankrupt every year. And the one thing you *can* bet on is that someone who urges you to put more money on the line is far more likely to profit from that decision than you are.

Remember, doing the same thing over and over again expecting a different result is the definition of insanity.

What should you do?

First, stop thinking of that lost potential profit as "your" money. It's not. It didn't happen, it doesn't exist. Maybe the whole market went down; if that's the case, don't panic-sell. Note that I *didn't* say "don't sell." You might want to sell—I don't know, every situation is unique. But I will stand by my assertion that you don't want to panic-sell. Go back and reevaluate the stocks and funds.

You could do worse than to follow Warren Buffett's wisdom, which he laid out in an annual letter in 2019, of the kinds of businesses Berkshire Hathaway looks to acquire:

> *First, they must earn good returns on the net tangible capital required in their operation. Second, they must be run by able and honest managers. Finally, they must be available at a sensible price.*
>
> —Warren Buffett

You're a grown-up; you get to make your own decisions. But emotions get in the way of making good decisions. Panic can be fatal. My experience is to stay with solid investments and continually reevaluate your positions, focusing not on the hype or what the rest of the market is doing, but on fundamentals.

## Setting Up Your Financial Plan

It helps when making decisions if there is a plan in place, and that the plan has been made for the right reasons. What are good reasons? Real, honest financial goals that take into account where you are in life, what you want to do with your money, your capacity for handling risk, and the things you do and don't want to do.

For instance, I have a friend who has read my book on making money in investment properties, *How to Jump-Start Your Way to Real Estate Wealth*. While he can see how well it can work to own an apartment complex, the last thing he wants to be is a landlord. It simply doesn't mesh with his personality or interests. And that's fine! He does other things to reach his financial goals. What's important is that you honestly take stock of your needs, your resources, and your personality.

What do you want, what do you have to help you get there, and how can you use your strengths to make it happen?

In my book *Retire and Refire*, I called this step a "Reality Check," and I offer up many examples of what it looks like. The plan you make must have a fighting chance of actually happening; you must focus from the very beginning on the reality of your situation. It needs to acknowledge where you are and lead you to where you envision yourself in several years, and even further into the future. It requires an annual assessment (if not more often) so that you can see if what you expected to accomplish actually happened. If not, why not? Did your circumstances change? Are new resources at your disposal? Where did things not pan out quite as you expected?

When you first make your plan, you're going to find that several of your assumptions don't pan out. That's not a problem! It just means you didn't have the best data. Regular assessments are invaluable because as time goes by, as you try a few different strategies, as you develop more skills (budgeting, investing, creative problem-solving), you inevitably gather better data. Use it to finesse and improve upon your original plan.

Let's look at it step by step.

## What Do You Want?

I promised I would talk about different portfolios, and this is where that happens. Because when you sit down to figure out what you want, I believe the first thing you will discover is that you want a bunch of different things! You want growth, but you also want safety. You want some money in the short term for one objective and more money in the longer term for something else. Then there are those medium-term projects, like sending a kid off to college. I'm sure other people will have different solutions, but what has worked for me is creating a different basket for each major objective.

I don't have one portfolio; I have a dozen.

I found early on that it was far easier for me to stay focused, to evaluate whether I was reaching my goals, when those goals were teased out and each given its own plan. You will have different goals for your money. You will be able to take different risks with it because those goals will involve different time horizons. You are choosing stocks on purpose to meet your goals, not grabbing things willy-nilly in a candy store because you like the pretty colors.

My family currently has $30 million invested in the stock market. I'm not saying that to brag. I'm telling you because if I can get here from arriving in California with $3,000 to my name, so can you. I'm proof of the pudding. I also want to be clear: If you think I can keep track of hundreds of stocks with that level of investment, you are wrong. As human beings, we have trouble with numbers greater than five! There's a reason your phone number is split into 3-3-4; try remembering a ten-digit string without breaking it up. It's not easy. What do I do with a portfolio of that size?

The same thing I do with my phone number. I break it into smaller chunks.

As a family, we divided that money up into smaller and smaller portfolios, and each one of those has a specific objective. The goal—education for my grandchildren, funding my retirement, developing a pool of money for a potential business investment, creating funds to go to causes we believe in—often comes with a built-in investment horizon. The stock market is not the place to put money you will need in a year or two. But funding a new grandchild's college education? You have at least fifteen years for that portfolio to grow. Retirement? If you're young, you may have thirty years or more. This allows you to weather the storms and take risks that, in the short term, might expose you to potential losses.

It's like having different sugar bowls that you keep cash in for different objectives: emergencies, vacations, a new car. Hopefully, your portfolio will have more money than a sugar bowl can handle, but the concept is the same. Your sugar bowls will be unique to you. You might, for instance, consider having portfolios to meet your future health needs as well as one for growth and another for security.

Whatever matters to you, creating a dedicated portfolio for each objective can help you stay focused. If you want a new car, start that sugar bowl! Keep that money separate from, say, your new house portfolio or your great-grandchild's education portfolio. Don't steal from yourself to gratify an immediate desire.

I understand that when an emergency comes up, you have to do whatever it takes. But true emergencies are happily rare. Don't live your life behind the eight ball or playing catch-up. Creating portfolios helps you define your priorities.

> *When it comes to the American Dream, no one has a corner on the market. All of us have an equal chance to share in that dream.*
>
> —J. C. Watts

Another reason not to try having one portfolio that must meet all your goals is that competing goals all tossed into one big pot will cause you to second-guess yourself when you need to sell or want to buy, or even when the smartest move would be to sit on your hands and do nothing. When you know what that money is earmarked for, it gives you a lens for decision-making that makes your choices clearer.

## How Many Individual Stocks Should You Have?

There are hundreds of industries and thousands of companies in the stock exchanges all over the world. You can't own a piece of everything. So how many stocks (or positions) do you want to have?

Let me start with a story.

I used to take my family to the Santa Anita racetrack. We'd pick our horses and cheer for them, and I'll be honest with you—I was more like the chumps in Coney Island than a savvy investor. No research was done ahead of time. It was gambling, except that we only put a couple of dollars down on each ticket. Our bets were for entertainment value only. There was no intention of getting rich at the races.

One day we went with a friend of mine, a great guy, and after every race, he would announce, "I won!" This went on, every race, until finally I asked him how it was possible for him to win every single race. The answer? He'd put $2 down on every single horse in the race.

My friend spread himself very thin. Yes, he had the pleasure of winning every race, but the cost of "winning" was far more than the amount I lost, and my horse never came in once that day. Sure, it's not quite the same as spreading your money over dozens of individual stocks you don't have the time or the bandwidth to research and monitor . . . but only because, at least in horse racing, one of those tickets was guaranteed to be a winner.

On the other side, if your version of my friend's strategy is to put all your money in a few ETFs and mutual funds, especially index funds, and go on about your life, I'm not going to tell you not to do it. Being diversified in that way, where someone else is doing the research or you're attempting to mirror the stock market at a low cost, is a pretty solid way to eventually get where you need to go. I'd rather see you more diversified than less. I have friends who have put huge stakes into a single stock only to have the company underperform, losing some or even most of their investment. That's a scary place to be. It exposes you to what I feel is too much risk.

I believe the optimum number of different stocks to hold depends on how many companies you can stay on top of. I know this is a book about wealth, but allow me to let you in on a secret: I don't think we want wealth as much as we want security. And how can we have security when we can't keep on top of our choices? Having a large portfolio with dozens of positions each worth $100 or $200—maybe it makes you feel like a mogul, but honestly, you're just making your life difficult. How can you make informed decisions on what to buy and what to sell if you have to keep track of fifty or a hundred different stocks? It's anxiety-producing. That's the opposite of the peace and security we think money will bring!

I think less is more.

Let's say you have an investment of $500,000. Maybe you want to own ten different positions. Diversification is critical, no matter how much money you have to invest. I would suggest having one index mutual fund or ETF to give you some built-in diversification, and then choosing an array of eight or nine individual stocks over several different sectors that meet your goal. Have twice that to invest? Double the number of stocks/funds to twenty.

You may have the same stock in three different portfolios; that's fine. Some stocks are appropriate to multiple goals. For instance, if it's a stock that pays an excellent dividend, you may want that in your income portfolio. These would be stocks that generate income to supplement your retirement savings, social security, and pension, so you would tailor it to positions that generate reliable income for you.

But remember that dividends can also be reinvested—maybe not in this portfolio, because you want the extra income to spend now, but in another portfolio that you have earmarked for long-term growth. You may also treat the stock differently depending on what that particular portfolio is for, selling over here where you would hold over there. Again, set up each portfolio deliberately, choosing a few targeted stocks and funds for each. Develop with intention. You are in charge.

As a final note, you probably won't be starting with a lump sum of $500,000. That's fine. Start where you are. Start with an index fund for diversification and one or two stocks that you've researched and believe in. Meet with your broker and have those strategic conversations now to help you reach that first milestone. You will learn so much by getting in the game.

## Write a Budget

Once you have decided what you want financially, which portfolios you're going to create and invest in, the next step is to put together a budget so you can start funding them. Where is that investment money going to come from?

This is where reality comes in. This is also where resistance shows up. I get it—if you thought making a budget was a fun way to spend your time, you'd have one already. But trust me, it is a crucial step. And it's a good bellwether, too: How much do you really want your financial goals? How much do you want to be comfortable, or wealthy, or be able to travel in your retirement without counting pennies? How much do you want the things you say are your dreams?

> *Every human being has a dream. I think what's special about the American Dream is that it implies . . . that there is the opportunity to make your dream come true. America signifies opportunity.*
> —Audra McDonald

If you don't want your dreams to come true enough to put the effort into making a budget, that is good information. You probably don't want them enough to do the research and sometimes make hard choices, including depriving yourself of things you may want in the moment in order to build a strong financial future. I'm not saying this to judge your choices, I'm saying it to show you that you have choices. And the first choice in front of you is to take this seriously and make a budget.

You can't know how to get where you want to go if you don't know where you are.

Let's get to it. How much money do you spend every month? Pull out your bank statements and your credit card statements. Go around with a notebook for a few weeks and write down all your cash expenditures. Take any big yearly expenses (property taxes, family vacation), divide them by twelve, and add that into your monthly budget. Data is your friend, so gather as much as possible.

Now take a look at how much comes in every month. What is your average monthly income from all sources? This is usually easier to figure out; we tend to have fewer income sources than outgo, and we have to do it anyway once a year for Uncle Sam. This part shouldn't take very long.

Moment of truth: Is there more coming in than going out? I hope so! If not, fix that first. Start by decreasing the outgo. What expenses can you cut? Go cold turkey on eating out, buying new clothes, and anything else that is purely discretionary—not for forever, but for right now. Take a hard look at any recurring charges; some of these may be for things you no longer need or use. If you haven't gone to the gym in six months, cancel it. I promise they will offer you a great deal to sign back up on January 1 and around swimsuit season every year. What's more important for you right now is to cut your expenses to a bare minimum. Stop the bleeding.

You should also increase your income: Get a second job part-time, rent out a room in your house, sell your art online. Your goals are, first, to have more coming in than going out, obviously, and then to create that six-month emergency fund that you can dip into when needed, including for working capital. But you can't dip into it if it doesn't exist.

If you do have more money coming in than going out, that's a great first step! When you have that and your emergency fund in place, the next step is to start paying yourself first.

You may have heard that term before. Here's what I mean by it: With every paycheck from every source of income, take 10 percent of it and put it toward your investment portfolio. Take it out of your bank account immediately, before any other bills are paid. An automatic option works best, so you never have to think about it. You're going to be making a lot of decisions; decision fatigue is real. Setting up an automatic transfer of 10 percent of your paycheck, every paycheck, into your investment pool (either with your broker or in a separate bank account just for that purpose) means you make that decision once and then never have to think about it again. Your investment pool just keeps growing.

Of course, this also means that your expenditures need to be 10 percent below your income. If that's already true, great! If not, go back to the beginning of this section and work some magic by both cutting your outgo and increasing your income.

You pay yourself first because the source of your wealth is your current paycheck. The greatest amount of money to fund your portfolio comes from paying yourself first. Start with 10 percent and consider increasing the percentage every time you get a pay raise. Your money will start to work for you almost immediately, but you have to pump money into the portfolio to start that virtuous cycle.

## Keep Track and Assess

You have to keep track of your investments to observe if there is appreciation or growth. This is where I find having multiple portfolios with different, clear objectives to be very helpful. I don't have to look at everything all at once; instead, I can look at my investments in discrete chunks. I set my expectations for both the short term and the medium term. What growth do I want to see in the next two months? What do I want to see from the company in terms of earnings or announcements in the next six months? How much growth do I want to see in a year?

> *Money won't create success. The
> freedom to make it will.*
> —Nelson Mandela

You must set up a schedule for assessing where you stand. Keep it simple and make it a habit. What are my goals for this pot of money? Are my investments meeting or exceeding those goals? What's the market as a whole doing? I can't expect my stocks to be increasing in value when the entire economy is in a recession. How am I doing compared to the S&P 500? Outside of the stock market, are my other investments (for me, that means real estate and private lending) doing as well or better? Always be looking for opportunities, if only to remind yourself that you have other options.

There's a pretty simple way to see how well you're doing, and if you need to do better, and that is the Rule of 72. Assuming you don't touch the money, your investment will double in a certain number of years. That number is 72 divided by whatever the annual percentage rate is that your money grows.

- If your portfolio averages 4 percent growth, your money will double in 72 ÷ 4 years, or 18 years.

- If your portfolio averages 6 percent growth, your money will double in 72 ÷ 6 years, or 12 years.

- If your portfolio average 10 percent growth, your money will double in 72 ÷ 10 years, or 7.2 years.

Obviously, you want it to double sooner rather than later, so it can start doubling *again*. And continuing to add money to the pot also speeds up the proceedings. The nice thing about this is that it works with any amount of money, so you can work backward. If, for instance, you plan to retire in twelve years and you want your retirement portfolio to be at $2 million by then, you have some real numbers to play with. If the portfolio is already at $1 million, it only has to average 6 percent growth per year for the next dozen years, and you don't have to add any other money to it for that to happen. As long as you have reliably been averaging at least that 6 percent growth with the portfolio, you're in pretty good shape.

But there is a BIG CAVEAT!

You can't time the market. If the economy tanks just as you retire, you don't want to need to touch that money—eroding your principal—until the market can recover. This is where diversification comes in. If your portfolio is on track, consider socking money into a different kind of investment, one that will tide you over if need be. Paying down your mortgage, for example, would mean one less big bill to pay monthly when you retire. Or beef up your cash and cash equivalents, perhaps increasing your emergency fund to cover more than six months of bills. Perhaps invest in real estate or in a side business so that it will generate income for you after retirement. There are many options, if you are already on track financially.

If you do the math and you're not on track—say your portfolio is at $250,000 and you want to retire in twelve years at $2 million in savings—well, that's very good information to have now, while there is still time to do something about it. You have options; don't panic. Don't start gambling. Stick to the fundamentals. But be honest about your situation.

First of all, you need to go back and look at your budget. Decrease your outgo now so you can funnel that money into your portfolio. Pay yourself as much as you can—don't stop at 10 percent. Get a second job now, something part time; it'll be easier to find and to take on at fifty-three than at sixty-five. What subject can you teach for money? What do your friends ask you to do for free that you could charge others for? What are your skills and talents? Any extra money that comes your way can go into your portfolio.

You might want to consider adding an index mutual fund so that you have something that mirrors the market itself, which has historically—over the long term—averaged more than 6 percent. Don't panic if the market goes down; it just means your money buys more shares of stock or of a mutual fund. Remember dollar-cost averaging? This is where it's very useful, taking the fear and emotion out of investing.

You may need to push retirement by a couple of years. You may need to downsize now instead of waiting until retirement so you'll have less overhead and more opportunity to sock money away. You may need to create a new income stream that can continue into your retirement.

The point is, doing a little math now saves you discovering you're going to be short of your goal too late to course-correct.

I don't want you to panic because I don't want you to put yourself emotionally in a position to make terrible choices—either to sell in fear or grab at something in desperation. What I want is for you to focus on numbers, on fundamentals, on reality. I want you to be *aware*.

Don't just jump from one shiny object to another; take the time to understand the underlying foundations of any investment. The more you know about the world you're trading in, the better your instincts will be. I have been lucky more than once, realizing my money could be better spent in real estate than the stock market or vice versa. But it's not really luck. It's that I am so plugged into both worlds that I can see when land prices are getting too high for it to be possible to make enough in real estate, for instance, to justify a new purchase. Or when I believe, because of my insistence on fundamentals, that the market is soaring too high, that it will soon become difficult to fulfill the ever-increasing expectations, and a bubble will burst.

For the last couple of chapters, I have hit hard on the notion of diversification, and while I hope I have convinced you to walk the talk when it comes to diversifying your stocks, you may have noticed that I myself don't seem to be a big believer in the other traditional diversification buckets. I don't like bonds, I don't keep 10 percent of my assets in cash, and I have sworn off precious metals. So, do I, in fact, diversify my own holdings?

You bet I do. The next section will show you how I do it.

# PART THREE

BEYOND THE STOCK MARKET

# CHAPTER TWELVE

## OTHER AVENUES TO EXPLORE

When I was around five years old, I went to work shining shoes. I enjoyed the work, I enjoyed having money, and I was good at it. Also, I was a little kid, so there weren't a lot of options for me to make money. When a beat cop chased me off and shattered my shoeshine stand, I was left without any way to make money. Because I had only that one source of income, I was exposed.

Now obviously I wasn't destitute. I was a five-year-old and my family took care of me; there was just a little less money for a while. We scrambled throughout the Great Depression. When I got a little older, paper routes, caddying, and other tried-and-true first jobs became available to me. But I did understand very early, and very personally, what it means to rely too heavily on any one source of income. I guess I've always believed in diversification, although I didn't always know what to call it.

*Don't limit investing to the financial world. Invest something of yourself, and you will be richly rewarded.*
—Charles R. Schwab

I am an advocate of having more than one job early in your life. You're young and you have energy, and a second job will allow you to build the pool of money you will need to invest. Getting a job in a coffee shop is fine, especially if it offers you benefits you aren't getting elsewhere, but starting a business of your own teaches you something priceless: that you can do things others value enough to pay for. You may also pick up organizational, time-management, bookkeeping, and lots of other skills that will serve you well as you grow in your career. It's also easier to move from one side business into another one without having to change careers or give up the steady paycheck from your day job.

I started out with a second job of doing taxes for friends and family. Then, as my real estate holdings grew, I spent more and more time managing those apartment complexes. I may be the first person to be thrilled to go from a second job of doing taxes to a second job of mowing lawns! But I owned those lawns, and that made a difference.

Isn't that one of the most wonderful things about America? We can work hard for other people, but we can also work hard for ourselves. And pride of ownership nudges us in a direction that makes everything better—neighborhoods, apartment homes, communities—for everyone else. It's a virtuous cycle.

## The Rule of Three

In terms of investments, I always use this rule: I look for three possibilities to do something useful with my money. I recommend this to you as well. It forces you to go slowly.

Don't jump at the first opportunity or shiny new stock. If you discipline yourself to come up with two alternatives, it forces you to take a longer look at that first opportunity. Maybe it is the best use of your investment funds; if so, you can move forward with more confidence, which might help you stick it out if there's a bump in the road. And if it's not the best use, then you know it before you've made the decision. It is easier to change your mind before you're committed to something. Explore your options. Stretch yourself.

This also helps you limit your risk. With financial wealth, you are not relying on your own exertions, but on other people. Sometimes human beings disappoint you. Companies go bankrupt, neighborhoods change, borrowers default. Higher rewards come with higher risks, and you will not always be on the winning side. But just like I told my kids, if I'm going to have one foot on a banana peel, I need to make sure my other foot is on solid ground.

I have not had only successes. What I've always had is a backup plan.

My stock portfolio has always been balanced by my diversification into real estate. More than once, I pulled most of my money from the stock market in order to buy a property, and then once the property started making money, I plowed that income back into stocks. I am very aware of both the stock and the real estate markets; when one gets overheated, I don't need to be greedy and hope it continues to rise. I can pull out of one—or both—and go into something else for a while. I don't flatter myself that I can time the market, but I do believe in having an awareness that you can take your profit and reduce your positions for a while—or at least pause buying, either land or stocks, when you have made enough.

So I always look for three different things to do with my investment pool. There have been outliers when an opportunity has presented itself, but for the last seventy years, my go-to areas have been stocks, which we have covered; real estate; and lending money.

## Real Estate

You may already be diversified into real estate in that you might own your own home. Congratulations! It's not a business the way owning a rental property is a business, but it is a source of wealth. It's also tangible property from which you can earn money. I know a couple who live in Augusta, Georgia, and make a good chunk of money renting out their home every year during The Masters golf tournament. You could also rent a room out to a college kid for an extra income stream or host live classes or workshops there (check zoning and business licensing laws in your particular neck of the woods).

Owning your own home is a primary source of wealth for most Americans. If you've read any of my other books, you know how much I love property ownership.

I have diversified primarily into real estate. That's worked well for me. I have found more than once that when the real estate market has been overpriced, it's been a good time for me to put my money into stocks. By the same token, I have pulled my money out of what I felt was an overvalued stock market and used it to buy an attractive real estate opportunity.

You don't have to go into real estate (although I wrote a whole book about how to do it if you want to, *How to Jump-Start Your Way to Real Estate Wealth*, if you wish to learn more), but whatever you do, having a powerful secondary way to build wealth is critical. You can't be at the mercy of a stock market sell-off.

# Lending Money

Once again, I started young. As a teenager, I noticed there were always some friends who were short before payday, usually because they were playing poker with their previous paycheck. I would lend them a few dollars, and when they got paid, they'd return the money with interest. These were very short-term loans, and they were my friends. Was there a risk they wouldn't pay me back? Always. But it only happened once, and the profit I'd made the other times was more than enough to absorb the loss. It was much more likely that they would pay me back because they knew somewhere down the line, they'd have to borrow from me again.

Still, once I moved out of the area, I stopped loaning money to friends. The difference between lending and gifting is that lending requires the money to be paid, usually with interest, while a gift doesn't. A successful loan is a business transaction undertaken in a professional matter. Which is why it's best to avoid giving loans to friends and family; those relationships are personal, not professional.

Lending can be seen as a service industry: You are lending someone money to fill a need. Usually loans are for covering emergencies, getting or staying in business, and providing for personal needs. Borrowers are at one end of the spectrum, and lenders are at the other end of the spectrum; they need each other, and both derive benefits.

I've held a lot of jobs in the financial world: I was an auditor with the IRS, I was an examiner for the state of California, I did people's taxes in the spring, and I gave workshops on money management through my church. I was also hired to be a manager at a credit union. What I always brought to the table was not just my expertise with numbers, but also my belief that everyone should be treated with respect. When I was auditing someone, my attitude was always that I was not there to "catch" them, but to work with them to make sure everyone was doing the right thing.

I won't sugarcoat it: I was hired by the credit union to help them with their loan program, but they were not honest with me. They didn't let me know the full extent of the problem until after I'd accepted the job—they had an extraordinary delinquency rate of over 30 percent. It was my personal philosophy that saved the day. I knew exactly what to do: I spoke to each delinquent borrower individually. We sat down together and figured out a budget that would take them out of delinquency.

I really don't believe people want to be delinquent on their loans, especially when they are part of a community. They were relieved to be offered a way out that was tailored to their particular situation. I helped them get back on track, and I helped them stay there with immediate calls if they were late with a payment. Some people need more help than others to stay on the path, but so long as everyone is treated with respect, they don't become resentful. In fact, these borrowers became our best clients, telling their friends to join the credit union. In three years, the credit union grew from $600,000 to $2,000,000; the dividend rate went from 4 percent to 6 percent; and the delinquency rate fell below 2 percent. I was very proud of the work I did there.

What it taught me was that there are people behind the numbers. Lending money isn't just about interest rates and credit risks; it's about helping people start or grow a business. If they have the need and you have the cash, it is possible to make loans to business people willing to pay a fair interest rate, knowing the loan will be absorbed as part of their business expenses. This isn't the same as lending money to a friend or relative who can never seem to make it from one payday to the next. This is a business involving written agreements, interest, and repayment plans. But if you have the financial skills and the people skills—and the money to lend—there are lots of ways into it.

Right now, I have a friend who owns a construction company. Some of his clients can pay for his services upfront, but not all of them have that kind of cash on hand. He offers them credit, creating a trust deed to secure the work that he's done, and I buy the contract from him. His clients get their lovely new patio or bathroom, my friend gets immediate cash from me, and I get interest and a higher value at the payoff. It's a win-win-win.

This is what I mean when I say you always have to be looking for opportunities. They are everywhere.

## Running a Private Lending Company

Loan brokers facilitate the lending business by finding borrowers and connecting them to lenders. They also have all the paperwork from the borrower prepared for the approval of a loan: the borrower's business plan, including their use of the loan; a loan application detailing personal and business history; a credit report; two years of tax returns; and a certified appraisal report for the security.

As a lender, you should be alert to the security of loan. If all the requested information has been reviewed and both lender and loan broker are satisfied, the loan can be approved. Legal documents to finance the loan are drawn up, and once everything is accepted and signed, the loan is made.

The real question with any type of loan is: Will it be repaid according to the agreement . . . or at all? A friend of mine said it best:

*It's easy to loan money.*
*The hard part is to get repaid.*

Through my experience in the Department of Corporations as an examiner, I was able to learn about lending the correct way. Later, as a credit union manager, I picked up the experience to actually run a loan program. Here's what I learned:

- The first step is to assess the character and history of the borrower by analyzing the application.

- Next, ask yourself if the security for the loan is acceptable. A key question to answer is, do you think it's probable that the borrower will be able to make repayments on time, given everything else going on in their lives, including whatever it is they're borrowing money to do?

- Next, make sure you fully understand the purpose of the loan. What is the ideal outcome of getting this loan?

- It's up to you to be able to evaluate the business proposal. Do you think this is going to work? The risk you believe is associated with their purpose in getting the loan is a critical factor in determining adequate security to protect the loan.

- Prepare the documentation if you decide to move forward.

Why would a borrower come to you when they could go to their bank? As a private lender, you are in competition with traditional lenders such as banks, savings and loans, and industrial loan companies. But here's the thing: Sometimes these institutions have impossible requirements for the lender. They might not understand the business or the neighborhood. They can take a long time to make a decision. They might charge exorbitant fees or prohibitive interest rates. Banks also have a lot more overhead than I do, for instance, and a lot more people who can say no.

I have found again and again that good people are turned down by traditional lenders. There is an opportunity for a private lender to make a decent loan with a fair interest rate, allowing a borrower to build or expand a business that serves them, their family, and the wider community.

It should go without saying (but I will say it anyway) that you need to carefully research any laws and licensing requirements that may exist where you live before you embark on professional lending.

## Trust Deeds

Remember that first stock, the Canadian Railroad stock, that I bought as a green kid in North Carolina? I sold it a few years later, in my senior year of college, to buy a trust deed from a real estate broker. A trust deed is a loan secured by real estate; think of it like a mortgage, but the loan can be from a private individual, not just from a bank. They're not as popular as they once were, but you can still find them in many states.

My mom was already investing in trust deeds and she put me onto this broker, who told me I needed to come up with $3,000 to buy the deed that would have a payoff of $5,000 about two years later. This was not difficult math to do: I would nearly double my money in two years, rather than getting just over 5 percent a year in dividends. It turned out even better than I had hoped: The man who owed the money ended up refinancing, paying off the note in full only a few months later. With that kind of return, it was no wonder that I turned my back on the stock market for a while and focused instead on trust deeds.

Trust deeds are loans. You lend someone, often a real estate developer, money for their project and they pay you interest monthly for a set amount of time. When the principal comes due, they pay off the deed in full. It can be a risky investment, so the interest rates are high, which means if all goes well, you have a steady stream of income over the course of the loan. On the other hand, there's no capital appreciation; as with a bond, you only get the face value back at payoff. So how did I get $5,000 back on a $3,000 loan?

Because the original lender needed money for something else, and trust deeds are not liquid. That deed still had two years left before it had to be paid back. The holder of the trust deed sold it for just over half its face value through a broker. He got the money he needed when he needed it, and I got the trust deed at a discounted rate.

If it sounds a little like junk bonds, you're not wrong; the mechanics are similar. The difference is that I grew up in a family who lived and breathed real estate. I was reading contracts to my mother as a child. I knew the landscape very well, and I also had my mother to guide me as she was investing in trust deeds as well. I had expertise, both hers and my own, to rely on. Finally, unlike junk bonds, a trust deed is based on a tangible asset: land. If the developer had defaulted, I could have foreclosed on his property.

I would be remiss not to warn you that there are sharks in these waters. As a child, I had seen lenders and real estate "partners" exploit loopholes that had bankrupted my mother. I have always tried to use trust deeds as a win-win. Either you are lending me money to help me buy property, or I am lending you money to help you succeed. So long as we treat each other with respect, every interaction—including buying the deed back early at a discount or offering you a deed in lieu of your commission—can serve both of our needs. But not everyone subscribes to my philosophy. It's important to find brokers you can trust and mentors who can help you spot any potential traps before you fall into them. But trust deeds are one way to make money from money, which is the essence of financial wealth.

## Loans on Vehicles

Later, I realized finance companies were financing vehicles at large interest rates and adding on extras like health and disability insurance to cover overhead—and frankly, to make more profit. To hide the financing charges, vehicle dealers raised the prices of the vehicles, then said there were no finance charges, when in fact, those charges had simply been absorbed into a higher base price.

There was obviously a way here to provide a better loan opportunity, as I had far less overhead and a different lending philosophy. The same rules apply to vehicle loans as in any other kind of loan: Study the application, know the purpose, evaluate the character of the borrower, check out credit history, assess reliability and the probability of payments. You do the paperwork through the dealer as though the dealer were making the loan. There are a lot of steps, and you should always check for local laws, but normally I have been able to lend the borrower up to 70 percent of the manufacturer's sticker price.

## Loans to Contractors

I mentioned that I've been working with a contractor friend. Properties are always needing contractors to do work . . . as plumbing, roofing, insulation, kitchens, bathrooms, patios, driveways . . . but people don't always have the ready cash to pay for it upfront. The contractor can offer a contract to do the work and finance the construction; they place a lien on the property for security.

Usually, the contractor's finance charge is at a low interest rate—it's an incentive to help them book the job. Unfortunately, it rarely makes financial sense for them to keep the contract; they need that money upfront to be able to pay their suppliers and crew. The contractor needs to sell the contract to recoup their costs of material and labor and pocket their profit. A private lender buys the contract from the contractor at a discount—that's where they earn their profit. That discount is built into the contract from the beginning.

It's up to the contractor to provide the application, explore the borrower's creditworthiness, determine the probability of repayment, etc. The lender here just purchases the existing contract. It is still up to the private lender to stay involved: You have to notify the owner, inspect the work performed on the property, determine the liens on the property, obtain the assignment of the lien on the property, obtain assignment of the contract, and file the agreement with the proper authority. It does help if you understand real estate. Caution: This type of loan is processed through an escrow company or authorized third party.

But for all the hassle involved, this may be my favorite type of loan. The owner of the property gets the needed work done, the contractor makes his living building something beautiful, and the lender makes interest on the loan. This is an arrangement whereby everyone comes out ahead.

## Factor Loans

There is a great opportunity to loan to borrowers who have produced products or are holding inventory. My father was in the garment industry, so I know it well. Manufacturers of production, such as the garment industry, produce garments, for instance, and until the wholesaler or retailer pays for them, the manufacturer must store and pay for their overhead—for which they may need a loan to tide them over.

All the same steps apply in factor loans such as the application, bank statements, credit reports, appraisals, etc. The loans are made on sales invoices or receivables as security, including their supplies or accumulated inventory. These are generally short-term loans based on the value of the production cost.

I don't suggest doing this outside of an industry you know as well as I know the garment industry, having grown up in it. You need to vigilantly inspect every aspect of production, inventory, even flooring, and you need a deep understanding of purchase contracts and sales potential.

Loans in these categories are very short-term and costly for the borrower; everybody, lender and clients alike, needs to really know what they're doing. Again, don't skimp on research to make sure you are in compliance with all local laws.

## Money Lending Can Lead to Wealth

There is significant financial wealth in being a money lender. I need only point you to the banking industry to show how well they (and many of the wealthiest people) do, simply by lending money. Appropriate short-term lending serves a beneficial purpose, helping people productively make their goals come true.

Many traditional finance companies and banks make loans at the most exorbitant rates. Their loans include shameless finance charges that take advantage of borrowers in need of money. This is especially true of credit cards, which are a form of money lending that many people don't even think twice about using. They have become a way of life despite being built on excessive interest rates and other fees. Most people really don't understand that buried in the contracts—also known as terms and conditions—are excessive loan costs that can keep them on a treadmill, never able to get ahead . . . much like my teenage friends playing cards, always losing and borrowing until the next paycheck and the next poker game. Adults should know better.

There is an opportunity for honest, reasonable private lenders to step into the breach. That could be you.

# CHAPTER THIRTEEN

## MISTAKES TO AVOID

Your mistakes, like your successes, will be unique to you and your circumstances. That said, there are some common pitfalls that you'll want to avoid.

## Don't Try to Go It Alone

Brokers have been the cornerstone of my success.

Whether we are talking about stockbrokers, real estate brokers, or loan brokers, it has been my privilege to work with a number of excellent partners—and I truly do think of these relationships as partnerships. When I see what I think is a good thing, I love having another smart, educated person to confirm that I'm on the right track or tell me to take a deeper look. One of the mistakes I made when I acted on that "hot tip" from my neighbor was to not be honest about it with my broker. He might have had insight that would have helped me better evaluate the mining company. It's true we learn the most from our own mistakes, but hopefully you will learn from mine and save yourself some time and money.

Find a good broker.

There will be lemons in the brokerage field as in any other field. I don't have time for people who seem to run on hot air. Move on. I will give you the same advice in these relationships as I do in the market: Go slowly. Work with someone, see if you understand each other, if you have the same investment philosophies. When you find someone smart and trustworthy, hang onto them. If they're talking over your head, that's on you. Ask them to clarify, get them to recommend books to read or courses to take. You must educate yourself so they can be a partner, not a guru; you must get yourself to the level where you can have an intelligent conversation before you can expect to develop a mutually respectful relationship.

I have to give a lot of credit to the many wonderful brokers I've worked with over the years. I had real estate brokers who kept an eye out for exactly the kind of property I wanted; they could spot a "Barbera" property a mile away, and when one came on the market, they made sure I was the first to know. Brokers have worked with me once I made an offer on the property, sometimes taking a note (or loan) for their commission if that's what it took to make the deal happen. Loan brokers have given me terrific opportunities to invest in trust deeds and helped me learn the ropes. I have benefited immensely from my stockbroker's expertise and advice, not to mention the advantage of having someone with experience helping me with the paperwork.

Some people don't know how valuable a broker can be, while others don't want to pay for a broker, but I have to tell you, the right broker will more than pay for themselves. Develop your relationships with brokers the same way you would anyone else: Ask friends for recommendations, have initial conversations, work together in a limited capacity as you discover whether or not this is going to be a productive partnership. If you're with an online broker, you might even have free access to a real human being who can give you, if not investment advice (we're all wary of that!), at least education and information about the potential choices and pitfalls ahead of you.

Brokers are not your friends; these are business relationships. But that doesn't make them any less foundational. You are only as good as the people around you. Take the time to invest in building relationships with experts. It has taken me far.

# Don't Leave Money on the Table

If you are working for someone else, check to see what perks they offer employees, especially regarding your retirement savings. For instance, many organizations will match up to a certain amount of your contribution to your 401(k) or 403(b) plan—sometimes right away, other times after you've worked for them for a while. It may not be a lot of money, but even if it's only $100 per paycheck, it's pure profit! If you put in $100 and they put in $100, your money has instantly doubled. That's 100 percent return on investment immediately, and you simply can't do better anywhere else.

Put as much as you can into these programs, up to the amount your employer will match. If you can put in more without compromising your other portfolios, that's up to you. The money is generally put into mutual funds, and you may or may not have some limited choice about which fund; they also often automatically become more conservative the closer you get to retirement. But none of that matters as much as the fact that, in addition to the average growth the fund will have over time, you will have your investment pumped up by your employer right from the start.

Take advantage of this and any other program your employer offers. A fifteen-minute chat with your human resources professional can have a significant upside.

# Churning

Churning is what happens when there's multiple buying and selling in short periods. As I mentioned toward the beginning of this book, in my early twenties I started doing a little day trading . . . until I was wiped out by that margin call. Lesson learned. As I became savvier, I took a longer and longer view of my stock market investments.

I came across churning when I was responsible for an investment account at the Pasadena City College Foundation. The investment decisions were made by a broker. In a period of six to eight months, he managed to grow the investment account from $50,000-plus to over $80,000. When I looked into how he did it, I realized that he held onto every share purchased only long enough for it to reach just a few points of increase, then he would sell. If it went down, he would buy again; if not, he would buy something else. I can't fault his short-term success, but this was a critical account. It wasn't play money. That kind of activity was too risky for me. I repositioned the investment account with another broker.

## Get Organized

You wouldn't run a million-dollar business trusting only your memory and piles of paper on the floor. Why would you think you could run what I sincerely hope will be a million-dollar investment account without a clear way of retaining, filing, and retrieving information?

Get out of your own way. Get organized.

I was very lucky in that my first wife, Bernice, was an absolute whiz at spreadsheets, crunching numbers, and organizing our investments. I did my part to keep contracts, estimates, paperwork, stock certificates, and everything else filed and easy to find. My work with the IRS also taught me the importance of always having a paper trail. Do yourself a favor and set up a simple system that can grow as your financial empire grows. Start as you mean to go on. You will never regret it.

## Self-Sabotage

Stop trying to outdo the market! Stop believing you know more of what is really going on than everyone else in the world. You will lose. The stock market is significantly controlled by the top wealthiest people in the country, top investment conglomerates in the U.S., and the government. They have so much money that when they start to move in or out of a position, they pull the market with them. "Word on the street," also known as gossip, is probably unreliable. Don't believe me? I have a hot tip for you on some mining stock . . . .

Selling, buying, or doing nothing are all choices. They all require thought and care. I suggest moving slowly; the market is filled with false rallies and shocks that send prices up and down and back up again, sometimes all in the same day, often within a week. Test the waters slowly. If there's a relative consistency down or up, stay with the winning activity. Don't try to outguess the trend.

If your stock or the market is on its way down, do something to make the best of the situation. Do you need to sell something at a loss to offset capital gains? Or maybe selling now gives you a chance to raise cash for a better investment. Or if you have a long horizon and believe the stock is fundamentally sound, hold your position until it rises again. You may even want to buy a stock that you believe has potential but has "gotten a haircut" in a down market.

If the market or stock is going up, again there is no one right thing to do. You might want to sell something you've been holding to take your profit. You might choose to buy stocks that are starting to recover from excess losses or jump into a stock that proved itself by withstanding the decline. Or you might want to stand pat.

There's a difference between choosing to wait and doing nothing. Doing nothing, ignoring the situation, is like sticking your fingers in your ears so you can't hear the bad news. It doesn't make the bad news go away. Doing nothing except hoping it will all work out (spoiler: it won't) is a recipe for disaster. Pay attention! If you see the market going haywire in either direction, simply take corrective steps.

Similarly, don't be driven by fear. After a sudden drop in the market, don't go into high gear trying to make up for the loss by piling in more money or going into higher-risk positions. If there are signs of a recovery, great! Keep on the same trajectory, considering the long-term investment strategy. The losses will be made up in time. Patience isn't just a virtue; it's a necessity.

Decide now to always take small steps. Revisit the decisions to see how those decisions worked out. Learn from your mistakes. Watch out for false bottoms or tops. See if there was a specific catalyst that caused the change in market value and act accordingly.

It's amazing how simple decisions become when you take the emotional weight off of them. Some stock investment did not increase? Accept that it was beyond your control. You did not have anything to do with it and you don't need to feel guilty, just sell and move on to another investment.

All my investments were structured for the long term. It turns out with all the ups and downs in the stock market, there is an overall force pushing the stock market up. Our economy and our profit-making corporations are constantly looking to correct hard times. It's in their interest to keep improving, creating better days for everyone.

Jumping into untried schemes to get rich fast generally falls apart. You don't need to get rich fast. Focus on getting rich slowly. If you want to gamble, play cards with your family for penny ante stakes. All the fun, none of the risk.

Don't bet with your future.

## Don't Forget to Reinvest Those Dividends

Nowadays, reinvesting your dividends is as easy as clicking a box in your online account. But oh, what a box to click!

Dividends are a great thing to have later in life when you need some consistent income from your stocks, and you don't want to touch your principal. At that stage of life, taking dividends as income makes sense. But as I alluded to earlier, they are even more important early in your investing career as a way to build up your portfolio without having to increase your direct investment. It's the stock equivalent of compound interest. Your stocks generate dividends, which are reinvested to buy more shares of stock, which generate more dividends. What's not to love?

You have to fill the well before you can start to siphon water out of it. Reinvesting dividends is a low-pain way to make a big difference over time.

## Plan for Things to Go Wrong

I think one of the worst things you can do is assume everything will go well. Me, I always assume something will go wrong. This is why you have something solid, something you can count on, running in the background. Lose your job? You already have a side hustle. Market going down? You still have rent coming in from the other half of your duplex. You are dollar-cost averaging by automatically investing a little money every week into your IRA so that when you retire, there will at least be something of a nest egg to make the transition easier. Planning for disaster won't prevent it, but it will soften the edges.

The corollary to that is that you shouldn't beat yourself up when things do go wrong. I wish we could control everything in life, but in fact, we control very little—other than how we deal with adversity. Show up as someone who knows they did their best and are prepared to keep doing their best. You'll make better decisions from that place, and that alone will help you get back on solid footing sooner.

## Be Aware of Bad Actors

There have been many prosecutions by the Securities and Exchange Commission for fraud, and there have been even more instances of managers, brokers, financial advisors, and others who seek to use others for their own gain. There have been problems ranging from Ponzi and pyramid schemes to insider trading to managers using fund assets as their own piggy banks.

*If it sounds too good to be true . . . it is.*

Follow no one blindly. Even those who are legitimately considered experts can be wrong; other times, they may be covering something up. Sadly, we learned in the 2008 crisis that even credit rating agencies might possibly have been influenced by companies to overrate their bonds; S&P paid a whopping $1.37 billion in a settlement with prosecutors. The way the business model is set up, it's the company *issuing* the bond that pays the credit rating agencies for their opinion about said bond.

*The three credit rating agencies were key enablers*
*of the financial meltdown. The mortgage-related*
*securities at the heart of the crisis could not have*
*been marketed and sold without their seal of*
*approval. Investors relied on them, often blindly.*
—Conclusions of the Financial Crisis Inquiry Commission

I'm not saying that credit rating agencies aren't full of people with high integrity, but I am saying they were found by the Financial Crisis Inquiry Commission in 2011 to have been "essential cogs in the wheel of financial destruction." It's impossible for an individual investor to do the kind of deep evaluations on every stock and bond that these types of agencies do all the time, but at the same time, it's a mistake to rely on anyone's opinion, even the "experts," without using your own common sense and due diligence. It's also a warning, once again, to be as diversified as possible.

## Stay Out from Behind the Eight Ball

I don't believe in buying things on installment plans—and that includes putting it on your credit card if you're not planning to pay your balance in full every month. Even with real estate, which requires bank loans to acquire, I'm always looking to pay off the mortgage early. I like living debt-free. It's such a struggle to constantly be trying to find the extra money needed for something you bought before you had the money to pay it in full, and the fees and interest associated with buying on credit mean that you are paying far more for whatever it is than you would if you walked in with cash in hand.

The biggest, most immediate bang for your buck that you can get is to pay off your debt. The emotional and financial freedom that creates will have an impact on everything in your life.

## Optimize Your Taxes

As a former IRS agent, I can tell you that we were trained to see the CORRECT tax was paid. Despite what you might imagine, the IRS is not trying to wring every nickel from you. Their job now, as then, is to make sure you are paying the correct, honest amount of tax according to the rules.

And there are a lot of rules.

Which is why you should take the following information as a brief and noncomprehensive overview and, I cannot stress this enough, talk to a tax professional about your specific situation.

Tax laws are constantly changing, and one reason is that the government wants to encourage certain behaviors by associating them with tax breaks and discourage other behaviors by creating penalties for them. You should not feel guilty about taking advantage of tax breaks; they were designed to encourage just such a behavioral shift.

## Different Types of Taxes

The first thing to understand is that not all taxes are created equal. Your income, for instance, is taxed at a different rate depending on how much income you have from your employer(s) as well as from royalties, alimony, rents, business, etc. The percentage of tax you pay is on a sliding scale; those who make more money pay a higher percentage in taxes than those who make considerably less money.

But there are also personal deductions that you can "take off" the income to lower your taxable income and sometimes even lower the percentage you pay (i.e., your "tax bracket"). These deductions range widely, from moving expenses to unreimbursed work expenses, childcare or dependent care expenses, charitable contributions, medical expenses, and many more, including:

- Tax-deferred retirement accounts

- Turning a hobby into a side business allows for deductions that are now business expenses.

- Rental property provides all kinds of deductions: depreciation, travel expenses, mortgage interest, repairs, and improvements. In addition, the property itself may show appreciation or equity buildup that can be greater than the rental cash flow.

- 529 college savings plans can accrue tax deferred.

- A Health Savings Account (HSA) might also be a tax-advantaged way for you to meet health expenses.

What does and doesn't count as a deduction shifts as tax law changes and may also depend on your circumstances. Again, I highly recommend seeking advice from a tax professional.

You might also get deductions or other tax advantages from your investments. Again, talk to a professional. I keep saying that, but the good news is, tax professionals are everywhere and likely dying to talk to you. Start with your employer or professional organization, then check with your bank or broker, including online brokers. They should all be very clear upfront about what advice they can and can't give you, but answering basic questions and pointing you toward more (and possibly tailored) information should be in everyone's wheelhouse.

## Take Advantage of Gift Tax Exclusions

There is a limited annual gift tax exclusion. Essentially, you can give up to a certain amount of money to as many individual people (including your children) as you wish, and that money is not generally taxed as income for the person receiving it. (The person should check with their tax professional, ideally before you make the gift.)

Be sure to stay within the limits in terms of all money given in a calendar year (including birthday and holiday gifts; keep good records). The limit is currently $18,000, but be warned, it is scheduled to go DOWN in the future. Always check before you make the gift.

Using the gift exclusion can be a strategic way to help your family. Because the exclusion refers to the fair value amount at the time of gifting, the key is to gift something that can grow in value over time. For instance, a friend of mine donated land to his grandchildren, planting trees in the grandchildren's names. When the trees matured, his grandchildren were able to pay for their college educations with the proceeds from the sale of the lumber.

## Planning Your Estate Tax

At the time of your death, if you leave behind a significant estate, there is an estate tax to be paid. This is also your last opportunity to make bequests to family and charities. Some folks say, "When I'm gone, what does it matter?" I think that's selfish. It is your responsibility to make sure the wealth you've created goes to good use.

The estate tax exemption in 2023 had a threshold for an individual of slightly over $13 million. If the estate is worth more than that, the balance is currently taxed at 40 percent. You might be like my friend who is happy to pay more in taxes, or you might want to endow some charitable institutions or take some other moves to reduce the amount paid in estate taxes.

You want to speak to an expert about creating trusts to ensure that your wishes are fulfilled after you've gone to the benefit of everyone you care for. States also vary in their inheritance taxes. At the very least, don't put off writing your will. Don't think of it as morbid; realize that it is a great kindness you can do for your loved ones to make sure everything is in order, so they don't have to worry about the future when you're gone.

# Don't Stop Learning

There are many books on the economy that may have been game-changers at one point, but they can quickly become outdated. This is because the economy is always shifting. Changes are sometimes enormous and quick, and at other times are ripples that ultimately reshape the landscape. New theories are always being developed to help us understand and take action. The following are books I have used to help me; they're not the only ones to read, but they're a good place to start.

- *Capitalism in America* by Alan Greenspan, Adrian Wooldridge
- *Mad Money* and *Real Money*, both by Jim Cramer
- *Hands Off* by Susan Lee
- *The One Minute Millionaire* by Mark Victor Hansen, Robert G. Allen
- *Beating the Street* by Peter Lynch
- *QBQ! The Question Behind the Question* by John G. Miller
- *7 Events That Made America America* by Larry Schweikart
- *The Death of Money* by James Rickards
- *Berkshire Hathaway Letters to Shareholders* by Warren Buffett

- *Unstoppable Prosperity* by Charles Payne
- *Against the Great Reset*, edited by Michael Walsh

# Philanthropy

Don't hoard your wealth.

Having wealth is not an end in itself. First, use it to take care of your family. Make sure your kids and grandkids get a first-rate education, ideally without the burden of student loans. Keeping your family safe and giving them opportunities isn't philanthropy—it's the foundation for them to lead a productive life.

Some people misunderstand charitable contributions as "giving back," as if you owe a debt. To me, obligation is not charity. Charity is freely giving to support people and causes you believe in. You give not because you are obligated to, but because you genuinely want to help.

> *The great use of life is to spend it for*
> *something that will outlast it.*
> —William James

A wealthy attorney friend of mine doesn't believe in charity. In fact, he would rather pay higher taxes and let the government take care of social needs. I questioned his choice of paying more taxes rather than giving generously to charities, which can be a deduction and mean he would be paying less in taxes. In the end, after taxes that year, we both had the same disposable income.

There is no right or wrong answer for either paying higher taxes or contributing charitably; surely both choices serve their purpose. But for me, charity comes from the desire to do good, to help the causes I believe in. Some philanthropists believe the greatest joy is to see the results in helping others. I don't see where the joy lives when my friend pays higher taxes. You get to decide where joy lives for you.

This stage of my life is focused on helping others. Another friend, also an attorney, suggested I set up a foundation. I took his advice and developed a portfolio to support educational programs that stimulate intellectual curiosity with critical thinking. I then designed programs myself that develop and equip people with values and virtues that matter to me, who in turn infuse those values and virtues into others.

This book was itself written to impart fundamental understanding so readers can become acquainted with different ways of approaching and making informed decisions in the paper world. I'm not doing it to be considered the new financial guru. On the contrary, I want you to read *many* financial publications for more information. I want you to do your own due diligence, talk to people with experience, and embark on lifelong learning. This book is obviously not technical or definitive; I waive any claim or guarantee as to any person's outcome from reading this. Your decisions are your own. But I hope that sharing my successes and failures helps you get a fuller picture of the world of financial wealth.

More than anything, I want to help you become the person you want to be. The ball is in your court. I recently read something that said, "If you want to be happy, make yourself happy." That really resonated with me. I jumped right up and took my wife, Josephine, out to lunch! It might have been a small thing, but it made me tremendously happy.

> *Happiness is not something ready-made.*
> *It comes from your own actions.*
> —Dalai Lama

You know what else makes me happy? That we have that power, that agency, to create our own happiness. It's up to us to make our dreams come true.

You live in the greatest country in the world. Your destiny is in your own hands. If you want to be wealthy, you can do it. It will take discipline. It will take hard work and sacrifice and owning your mistakes. But it can be done. You can create the life you want.

I believe in you.

# CHAPTER FOURTEEN

## MY PERSONAL PHILOSOPHY

There are many reasons to develop wealth. I won't lie to you—a certain amount of happiness comes from having wealth. But beyond the human desire we all share for housing, food, and having our basic needs met, it's not what money can buy that matters. There is a satisfaction, a quiet joy, that comes from the accomplishment of meeting your goals, of making good choices, of being in control of your own destiny. That joy is added to when you do, in fact, have enough money to relax, see the world with the people you love, give generously to causes you believe in, and make sure your family won't struggle after you're gone.

Having enough for all of this allows you to be generous and expansive in your worldview, and that brings tremendous feelings of connectedness. It gives you peace of mind, a chance to be part of the bigger human picture, that you simply can't access when you are worried about making rent. For your good and for the good of all humanity, I want you and everyone to be able to access wealth. I have done my best with all of my books to outline different ways to make that possible.

Now, I want to give you some advice on the different mindsets and attitudes that I have found most helpful on my own journey from shoeshine boy to multimillionaire. I don't say this to brag; I say it to let you know that if it was possible for me to go so far in my life, it is also possible for you.

First, embrace time.

No matter where you are in your life, embrace time as an ally in creating wealth. We live longer now—we have more opportunities than ever to experience the world and to make decisions that will reward our future selves with security and serenity. Any amount of money that you can sock away today in something that will appreciate at a rate above inflation is a good start. Starting immediately matters more than starting perfectly; your money can grow while you educate yourself. Besides, there is no better education than getting in there and getting your hands dirty, making mistakes, and learning from them.

I believe that creating wealth is part of a healthy lifestyle. Not a point of view you may have heard much! But hear me out: The mental agility to always be looking for opportunities to invest keeps you mentally active. It requires you to develop discipline and self-control. There continue to be new mental challenges and lifelong learning as innovations in technology change the game. Networking and developing personal relationships are critical steps, and there's plenty of data to show that a healthy network of human connections is one of the best things we can do to increase our well-being as we get older. It's fully engaging to balance the wisdom of what you've learned, "old-school" experience, with the ever-changing landscape of the current financial environment. It keeps me active, it keeps up the spirit of staying alive, and I think it will do the same for you.

I don't believe in total retirement. I'm in my nineties now, and I've never believed that my life should be limited as I grow older. I learned that from my parents, and likewise, I am happy to see my children taking the same path.

When people ask me what I do and I tell them I am an investor, they tend to be dumbfounded. I think part of that comes from a misunderstanding of what it means to be an investor. To me, being an investor is a perspective, a lifestyle. It is using money to make money. Nothing could be more different from working for a paycheck. As an investor, you are independent, unsupervised. You are free to make your own decisions. And you are 100 percent responsible for your choices.

*The buck stops here.*
—Harry S. Truman

You have to stay sharp. It is up to you to take advantage of opportunities and to get back on your feet if you fail. You can't let failure stop you. You can't let it mean there's something wrong with you. If you see it instead as an opportunity to learn from your mistake and do better next time, you are setting yourself up for success. I have to tell you, it feels so much better to live with your mistakes (at least when you're willing to learn from them) than it does to have a boss you need to apologize to. When you invest for yourself and family, the stakes are high, but I believe it is a challenge you can rise to with critical thinking and a willingness to learn.

My goal was always to reach the Sweet Spot: to have enough money invested so that my investments would generate enough yearly income for me to be financially independent. You may not get there right away, but you can get there. Take stock of your assets, and I don't just mean your stock portfolio. Where can you create streams of income? Can you work part-time or monetize a hobby or creative enterprise? Can you rent out a room in your house or sell some junk in your garage? Being able to add just a little more to your investments or leave them untouched a bit longer or need a little less can be the thing that tips you over into the Sweet Spot.

It's not about denying yourself; on the contrary! My late wife, Bernice, and I found such joy in coming up with free ways to have fun together. It became a game. If you don't think of it as depriving yourself, but instead as investing in yourself, it all becomes much easier.

My own success was built with the help of many people: family, like-minded friends, professors, and mentors. I am always learning from successful people in all walks of life. I'm fortunate to have met several presidents of the United States and other politicians, presidents of colleges, business owners and founders, and many wealthy people. When I meet successful people, I am in awe and humbled to be able to talk to them. Without fail, they have been gracious and shared their insight. They all earned their status and energized me to do better.

You, too, can look around you and see who is a step ahead of you on the road you want to travel. Be appreciative and humble and let them offer you their insight. For me, what matters most is not their net worth, but their character: Do they have humility, kindness, and truthfulness? Conversations and relationships with that kind of person are worth their weight in gold.

That is my personal philosophy. Now, let me sum up the principles I have developed that have guided my success over a lifetime of investing.

# Timing

One of the most important lessons I learned from my dad concerned timing. I don't mean trying to time the market, which is not a strategy I recommend. No, the kind of timing I'm talking about is that of understanding that there is a time for everything in nature, in the stages of our life, and also in our investment strategy.

There will be times when the economy as a whole is going forward and times when it is going backward. Certain industries will rise and fall on their own times. You can't stay stuck in one (and only one) path. You have to be looking for the best opportunity in whatever time you're in. When there was a mass migration to go west for gold, pioneers staked claims and risked their lives. Many ended up as broke after the Gold Rush as they were before. The smart guy didn't risk his life digging or panning for the big score; instead, he sold shovels, picks, clothes, and maps. His profit margin wasn't the same as striking it rich, but time and volume were on his side.

A safe portfolio isn't exciting. It doesn't make for great dinner party conversation. In fact, people might even make fun of you. But when you retire with no financial worries because your investments have grown steadily, you'll have the last laugh.

# Flexibility

The next thing I learned to cultivate in my life was flexibility. I focused on reinventing myself again and again. What happened in the past, who I was or what job I had—that's not how things have to be. Not for me and not for you. For every door that closed on me, I kept looking until I found another one open. Don't think I've never failed or been lied to or stayed too long in a position where I wasn't valued. Of course I faced all of that, just like you will. But I succeeded by not letting those moments define me.

> *I believe in America because we have*
> *great dreams, and because we have the*
> *opportunity to make those dreams come true.*
> —Wendell Willkie

I was always on the lookout for better. I succeeded by repositioning myself. I changed careers many times, from being an auditor in the Internal Revenue Service to being an examiner for the state of California. I sold cars, I ran a restaurant, I was a loan officer in a bank. One day, a new acquaintance told me that my personality was better suited for being my own boss, and he was right! I made less money in the beginning, but I was disciplined and focused and very soon I took off.

One look at nature will show you how life itself is constant change. You have to change right along with it; if you don't adjust, you lose. Reinventing yourself can be exciting. The key is to always be reevaluating as circumstances change. Stay flexible.

# A Positive Mindset

Look, you can be positive or negative no matter what happens to you or around you. It's your choice. But it has been my experience to see that when you choose to be positive and optimistic, you will have better outcomes than when you choose to be negative and pessimistic. You will make better decisions; at the very basic level, you will be more likely to move forward when you are optimistic than when you are pessimistic.

Forward motion means some progress, and we are all for progress! You learn when you keep moving forward. A negative outlook has no energy to it, no initiative. Sometimes the best move is to turn a negative circumstance into positive possibilities. When you are negative and pessimistic, you can't see the light in those darkest hours. You don't take chances, and you stay stuck. I've had investments that have gone sour, but there is a wide difference between having an exit strategy and giving up.

What is in your control? What isn't? Where can your efforts turn the situation around? Success isn't hanging onto a stock when it is plummeting, hoping it will go up. Success is evaluating the foundations, owning up to mistakes, not being greedy (in other words, take your profit when it's enough; don't assume it will always go up), or if you still believe in something that isn't doing well, having the financial flexibility to be able to give it time to recover. Not putting yourself in a position to have to make desperate choices is as much mindset as it is having an emergency fund. If you are addicted to drama, chances are your investment portfolio and "strategy," if you can call it that, will involve too much drama. Boring profits are good!

## Share with Others and Learn from Experience

We learn best from our own mistakes. If, that is, we are willing to look at them dispassionately. Put blame aside. Devote your entire life to learning. You are never too old or too successful to learn something new.

*The more you know, the more there is to know.*

Information is sometimes elusive or abstract; hearing from real people how they navigated the problems you are facing, or are likely to face, can make potential solutions concrete. If you are lucky enough to find people willing to share their advice, for heaven's sake, take it! By the same token, be generous with your own advice. We are all in this life together.

# Loyalty

Loyalty is a core value of mine. It requires a relationship of both trust and forgiveness. Trust, because you need the freedom from suspicion, which is poisonous to relationships. Forgiveness, because no one is perfect. It is a sign of mutual respect to accept the foibles of our family members and friends, and for them to accept ours. So long as there is no malice, wonderful relationships can blossom.

Loyalty can be the foundation of truly extraordinary accomplishments. I am so proud to have worked with three generations in my family, in our businesses and in our investments. Mutual respect and loyalty—not blind trust, but well-earned loyalty, like-minded goals and decisions—have been the hallmark of our family's success.

# Goals

For goodness' sake, have a goal! Have more than one goal. They don't need to be the same as my goals or anyone else's. Having a goal focuses your attention and helps you make aligned decisions. It actually helps you develop a good process, which is fundamental. Plan to reach your first goal. Fulfill that plan, improvising when necessary, learning all the way. Then move onto your next goal, and your next. Goals are just milestones on the bigger road to success.

Perhaps the most important principle I follow is my belief that reaching each goal is important, yes, but how you reach it, the individual responsibility you take to make it happen, is how you build character. And your character ultimately defines your life. For all the obstacles that come along, and there will be many, your success will be all the sweeter knowing you were able to bring people along with you, that you followed the rules, that you were generous and kind along the way. Destiny will take care of itself.

I hope this book has helped you begin to develop a fundamental understanding of financial wealth in some of its many forms. Of course, this was just meant as the beginning of your journey. It's not a technical or definitive book, and I hope I have disclaimed often enough that you need to do your own research and make your own decisions.

Your mileage may vary. But I wanted to give you a framework as you dive deeper into this world.

I wish you a journey filled with health, happiness, and wealth.

# Acknowledgments

Any acknowledgment must start with my family. When I hear Frank Sinatra sing, "I did it my way," it always gives me a great thrill. I have a lifetime of appreciation for my wonderful family, all of whom have helped me over the years to, in fact, do things my way.

From my dad, John, I learned to be independent, to learn a craft that would always keep me in demand. When trouble came along, I learned from his example to be patient. I remember him telling me how taking your time can result in saving a great amount of energy and mistakes down the line. Other words of wisdom from my dad included "Don't worry, it can be solved," which is a good philosophy with which to approach any problem, and of course the classic "Just mind your own business."

From my mom, Rose, I learned to be vigilant and enterprising. She wanted me to "strike at every opportunity" and to "always be a producer." She also encouraged me to work hard: "The streets are not paved with gold, and money does not grow on trees."

My brother, Henry, set the example of being a lifelong learner. "Education is a lifetime necessity." Henry became a college professor, respected in his field; he often edited his fellow professors' material and papers in sociology. Together, growing up, we were in love with our library. It was our candy store.

My mom had a third-grade education, and my dad had a fifth-grade education. But their common sense had no equal. They watched over me and Henry in the down times and led by example, showing us the right thing to do. Our family was always independent, minimizing expenses and too proud to apply for welfare programs even during the Great Depression. Ironically, we always stayed hungry—which provided the impetus to always do more.

My first wife, Bernice, to whom I was married for forty-five years, accepted my faults and trusted my choices. She kept us together as a family and saw to the needs of our children and grandchildren. Ours was a marriage of shared respect, right up until the day she passed away.

I am also blessed by my wife of twenty years, Josephine, who reminds me that life is good. She keeps me organized and has an uncanny intuition, able to see trouble ahead. Both my wives have given me a full life, wonderful companionship, and the ability to appreciate life's wonders. They also kept me from making so many mistakes; I would never have succeeded without their support.

My children, Ann, John, and Pat, have followed in my footsteps, which is possibly the greatest acknowledgment a father could hope for. In their own way, each has contributed to and sacrificed for our family and our family business. They have also been wonderful parents to my beautiful grandchildren. In these troubled social times, I am so proud that my children and grandchildren lead clean, productive lives and remain family oriented.

I have also been fortunate to have some wonderful mentors over the course of my life. I have had great teachers, especially Dr. Moore at Los Angeles State College. As head of the accounting department, she appointed me as a reader and directed me to a career in accounting, which laid the foundation for so much that came after.

I want to give thanks to the directors of the nonprofits I am involved in, namely Ina Cohen of Lingua Viva, an Italian language class; Simone Schiavinato of *L'Italo-Americano*, the oldest Italian-American newspaper in the United States; Catherine Miller, artistic director of the Pasadena Vocal Competition; and Kate Richardson of Society for Sister Paula.

I would be remiss in a book of this nature not to give thanks to my broker investment team, including my real estate brokers over the years, who brought me great deals and helped me make them work; my stockbrokers for their outstanding performances and help with my investments; and my other general investment advisors, all of whom I have learned from.

My thanks to the wonderful Laura Brennan for editing all five of my manuscripts. I also want to thank the many manuscript authors and editors of the fifty Mentoris books, with special thanks going to Karen Richardson, the super director of the Mentoris Project.

At various times, friends have given me advice that I treasure, while mentors have freely helped make my world a better place. So many people have provided me with constructive relationships, leading to opportunities I would not have been able to realize on my own. Even the occasional jealous acquaintance has sharpened my decision-making. Thank you all.

More than anything, I appreciate that opportunity is everywhere. You just have to look for it. To accomplish what I have managed over my life—that has offered me the greatest joy.

# ABOUT THE AUTHOR

Robert Barbera is proud of his immigrant parents. They taught him the value of hard work and the importance of family. He made his first stock investment in 1954, only four years out of high school, and bought his first building in 1961. Through hard work, dedication, focus, and the support of his family, he now has 500 units and multiple subsidiary companies, making real estate the cornerstone of his success.

Throughout his life, Robert has built wealth not just for himself and his family, but for many other people in fields as diverse as restaurants, car dealerships, and the financial industry. He launched The Barbera Foundation in 1994 and has donated his time, expertise, and financial resources to many worthy organizations, including Pepperdine University, Thomas Aquinas College, and the California State University system.

Robert was lucky in love, having had a happy, forty-five-year marriage to his late wife, Bernice, and finding love a second time around with Josephine, whom he married in 2003. He is the father of three wonderful children, Ann, John, and Patricia, and the grandfather of seven.

The Mentoris Project represents a piece of Robert's legacy. It connects his past, his parents, his children, and the future by honoring the achievements of Italians and Italian-Americans, by sharing his expertise to help people create wealth and make the most of their assets, and by publishing inspirational books. Learn more at www.mentorisproject. org.